# Creating Extraordinary Beads
# from Ordinary Materials

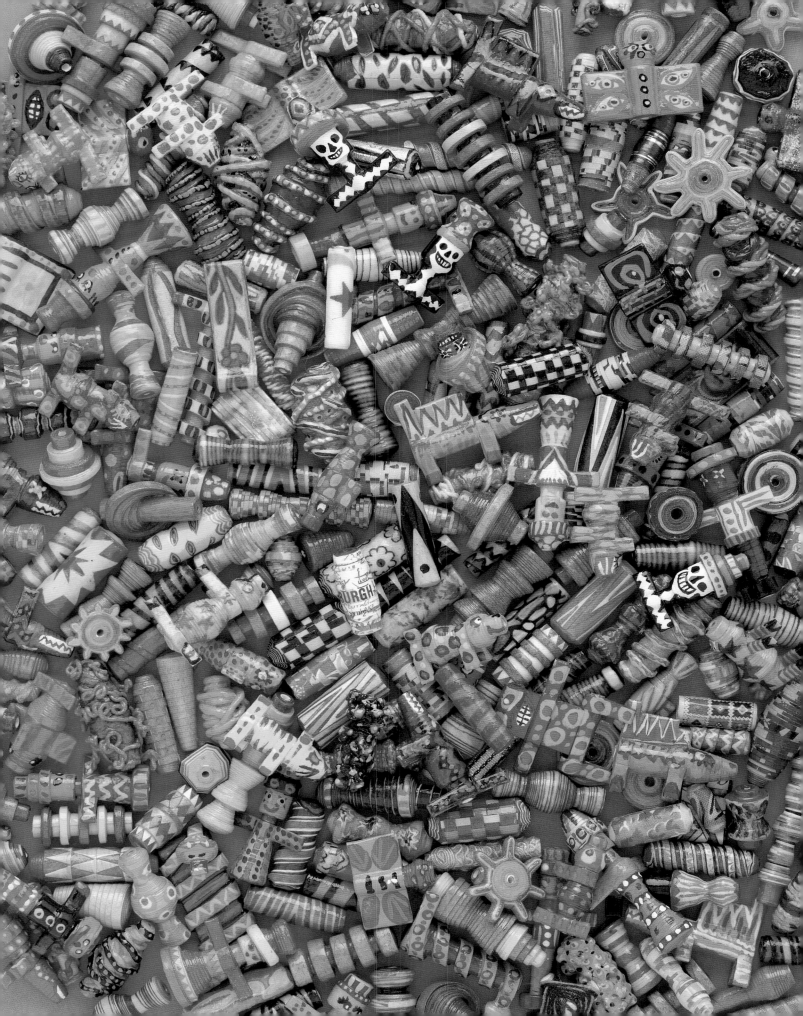

# Creating Extraordinary BEADS From Ordinary Materials

## TINA CASEY

**NORTH LIGHT BOOKS**
Cincinnati, Ohio

# About the Author

Tina Casey has been a passionate lover of beads since her childhood days in Pittsburgh, Pennsylvania. In the early 1970s she experimented with many different forms of seed beadwork, including looming, applique and lace. After a twenty-year detour through a B.A. in Philosophy at Columbia University, one career as a professional seamstress, another career as a press officer for the New York City Department of Environmental Protection, and still another as a freelance arts and crafts writer, she landed in New Jersey as a full-time mother and finally realized that she could obtain an infinite variety of beads quite easily, and cheaply, by making her own.

To develop the projects in this book, Casey drew on the lessons of her parents, both of whom are teachers, artists and craftspersons. They raised three children to respect the earth and the materials it provides, and to find the inner beauty in even the most crass of these. They instilled in her the drive to explore freely, experiment boldly, perfect relentlessly and communicate joyfully.

Casey's crafts articles have appeared in *Parenting Magazine* and *Family Life*. She has taught paper bead design in the New York area, including workshops for the New Jersey Center for Visual Arts and the Bead Society of Greater New York. As if possessed, she continues to invent new paper bead designs.

Other fine North Light Books are available from your local bookstore, art supply store or direct from the publisher.

01  00  99  98  97      5  4  3  2  1

**Library of Congress Cataloging-in-Publication Data**

Casey, Tina.
    Creating extraordinary beads from ordinary materials / Tina Casey.
        p.      cm.
    Includes index.
    ISBN 0-89134-763-1 (alk. paper)
    1. Beadwork. 2. Beads. 3. Paper work. I. Title.
TT860.C37   1997
745.58'2—dc21                                          97-3649
                                                            CIP

Edited by Joyce Dolan
Production edited by Marilyn Daiker
Designed by Angela Lennert Wilcox
Cover photography by Brian Steege, Guildhaus Photographics
Introduction and chapter opener photography by Hal Barkan, BKT Photography

North Light Books are available for sales promotions, premiums and fund-raising use. Special editions or book excerpts can also be created to specification. For details, contact: Special Sales Manager, F&W Publications, 1507 Dana Avenue, Cincinnati, Ohio 45207.

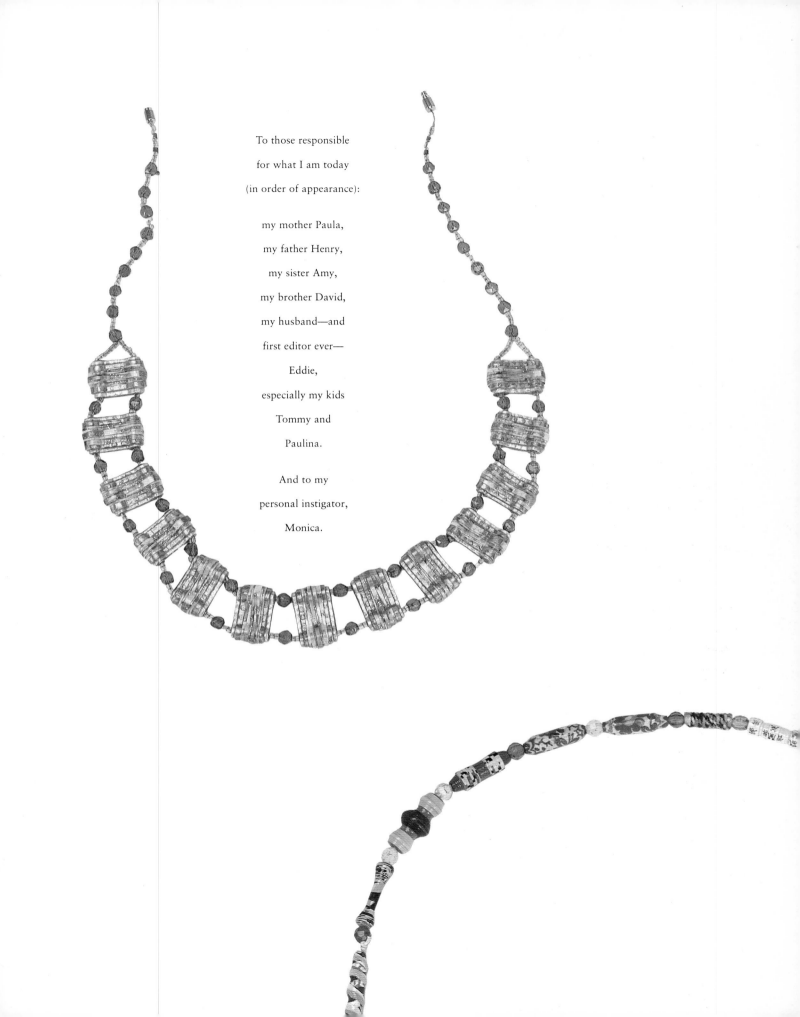

To those responsible
for what I am today
(in order of appearance):

my mother Paula,
my father Henry,
my sister Amy,
my brother David,
my husband—and
first editor ever—
Eddie,
especially my kids
Tommy and
Paulina.

And to my
personal instigator,
Monica.

# Table of Contents

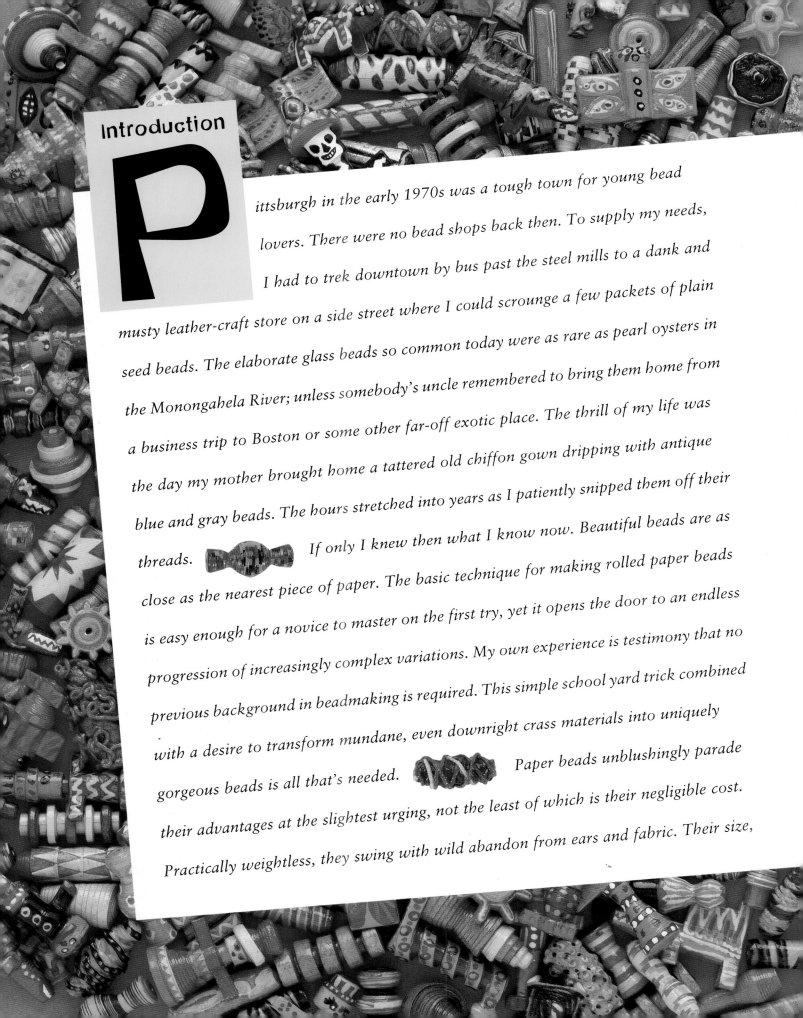

## Introduction

**P**ittsburgh in the early 1970s was a tough town for young bead lovers. There were no bead shops back then. To supply my needs, I had to trek downtown by bus past the steel mills to a dank and musty leather-craft store on a side street where I could scrounge a few packets of plain seed beads. The elaborate glass beads so common today were as rare as pearl oysters in the Monongahela River; unless somebody's uncle remembered to bring them home from a business trip to Boston or some other far-off exotic place. The thrill of my life was the day my mother brought home a tattered old chiffon gown dripping with antique blue and gray beads. The hours stretched into years as I patiently snipped them off their threads. If only I knew then what I know now. Beautiful beads are as close as the nearest piece of paper. The basic technique for making rolled paper beads is easy enough for a novice to master on the first try, yet it opens the door to an endless progression of increasingly complex variations. My own experience is testimony that no previous background in beadmaking is required. This simple school yard trick combined with a desire to transform mundane, even downright crass materials into uniquely gorgeous beads is all that's needed. Paper beads unblushingly parade their advantages at the slightest urging, not the least of which is their negligible cost. Practically weightless, they swing with wild abandon from ears and fabric. Their size, shape and color easily adapt to the desires of their creator, whether it be to complement manufactured and antique beads, jewelry findings, clothing or accessories—even lampshades and other home furnishings. Many other crafts, like macramé and weaving, also prove to be fertile ground for designing with custom-made beads. 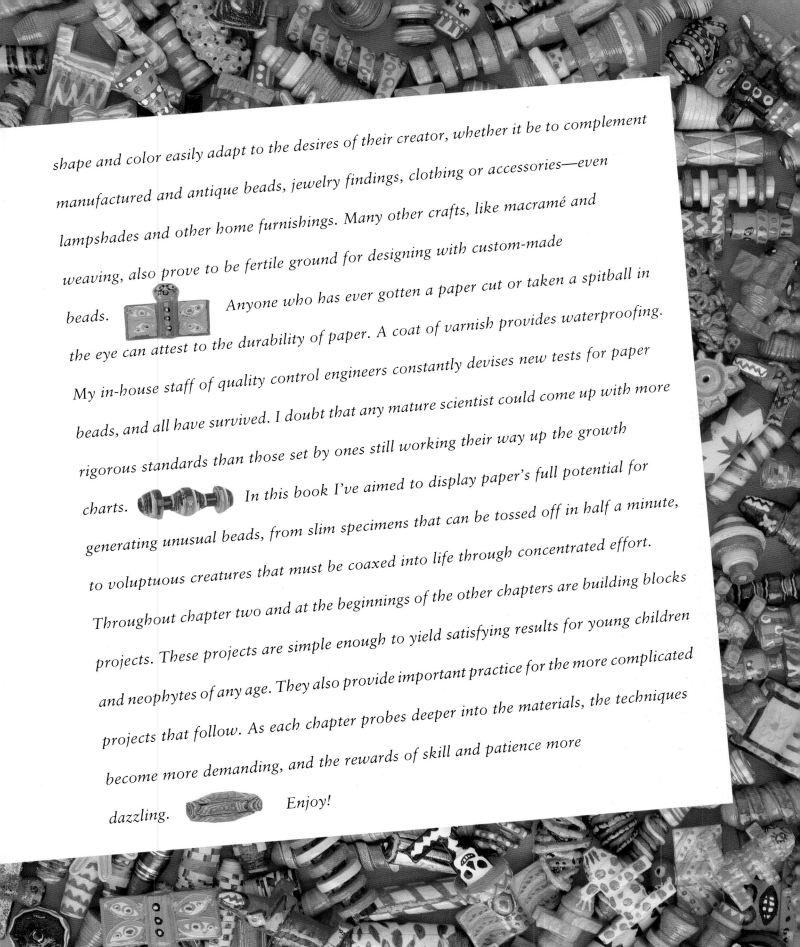 Anyone who has ever gotten a paper cut or taken a spitball in the eye can attest to the durability of paper. A coat of varnish provides waterproofing. My in-house staff of quality control engineers constantly devises new tests for paper beads, and all have survived. I doubt that any mature scientist could come up with more rigorous standards than those set by ones still working their way up the growth charts. In this book I've aimed to display paper's full potential for generating unusual beads, from slim specimens that can be tossed off in half a minute, to voluptuous creatures that must be coaxed into life through concentrated effort. Throughout chapter two and at the beginnings of the other chapters are building blocks projects. These projects are simple enough to yield satisfying results for young children and neophytes of any age. They also provide important practice for the more complicated projects that follow. As each chapter probes deeper into the materials, the techniques become more demanding, and the rewards of skill and patience more dazzling. Enjoy!

CHAPTER ONE

# Tools and Materials

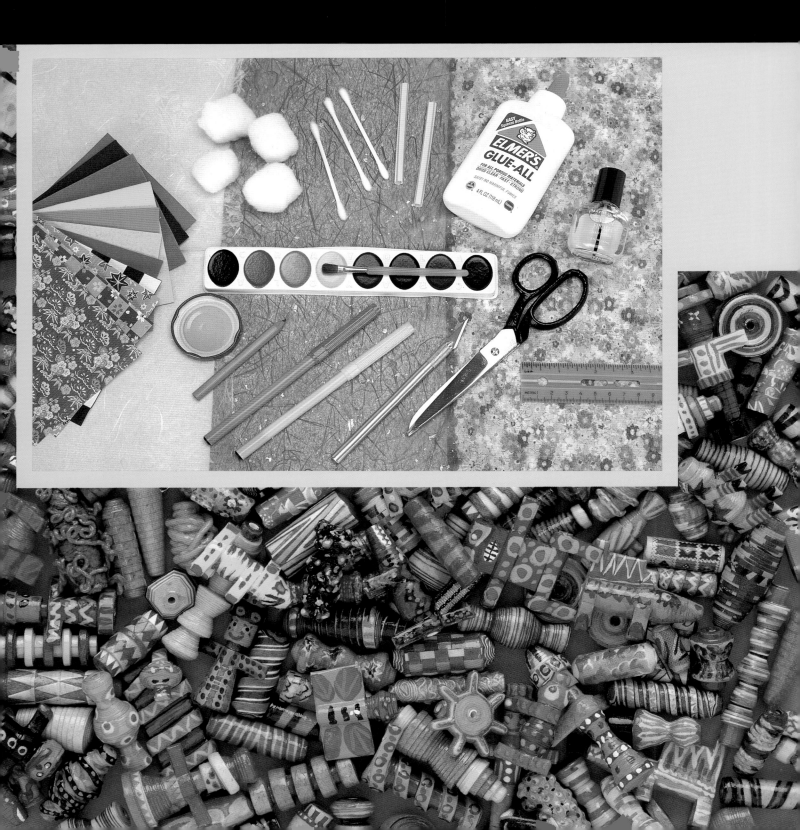

**W**ith only paper, a slim stick, glue, paint and scissors at hand, an astonishing variety of beads springs to life. In addition to these basic supplies, the choice of tools and materials is merely a matter of convenience, even more variety, and craftsmanship. I've engineered this book so that a bit of foraging around the house, and possibly a trip to a local supermarket or general merchandise store, will provide everything needed to make all of the projects.

**Paper Examples** Beautifully designed paper is not a prerequisite for a beautiful bead. The top three beads in this group are made with lush, origami paper, but the bottom four are as interesting, and they're made with a blue and brown grocery bag, a red and yellow label from a can of tomatoes, a road map, and bright red, white and blue paper from the outer layer of a bag of kitty litter.

## The Stick

Paper beads are made by rolling a long strip of paper around a slim stick. Any stick. For consistency, I use hollow plastic cotton swabs throughout this book. They come in a standard size, are widely available and they're cheap. Because they're plastic, it's easy to pull them out of the finished bead. They're hollow, so they can be trimmed and left inside the bead for extra durability.

Plastic coffee stirrers and drinking straws are other options, but virtually any slim stick can be used. However, if glue or shellac gets on a wooden stick, like a toothpick, it can wedge stubbornly inside the bead, making it useless for anything but an extravagantly decorated toothpick. The same problem can beset nails and other metal sticks.

## The Paper

Colored construction paper is used in most of the projects throughout this book. Thick paper like this type is important for building the dramatic silhouettes of many of the beads. Heavy paper shopping bags are a good substitute.

Plain white typing or photocopying paper is used for some of the projects in chapter two as is a variety of *found* decorative papers, such as colored newspaper advertising headlines, gift wrap, canned food labels and catalog photographs. Any kind of paper is potential bead fodder, but avoid paper that is stiff or has a hard, glossy finish. It can be difficult to roll smoothly and may not hold glue.

Some of the textured beads in chapter six call for tissue paper—the kind that comes in gift boxes. Many other kinds of very light, soft paper can substitute. Paper napkins, paper tablecloths and especially crepe paper are good sources for colored tissue.

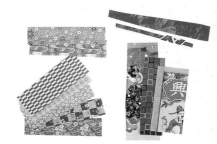

**Decorative Paper** The increasing diversity of cultural life in the U.S. is a bonanza for paper bead makers. The geometric patterns on the left are colorful Japanese origami paper, widely available in art and craft shops in this country. The floral designs are also origami paper, carried by a Japanese supermarket in New Jersey. An Asian neighborhood grocery in Oregon had shelves of goods packaged with lavish illustrations, like the one on the far right.

## Nail Polish

A coat of varnish is needed to waterproof and give the beads a shiny finish. Clear nail polish will do very well. Please see Finishing Touches, page 14, for further explanation of varnish's effects on beads.

## Scissors

Scissors are required for all of the projects. Any decent pair will do, even children's safety scissors.

## Glue

Any kind of glue is fine—white glue, paste, mucilage or rubber cement. Glue sticks tend to be awkward, however. I prefer white glue. I pour it into a small dish and brush it on with a small paintbrush. This is quicker and more accurate than squeezing it directly onto the paper from the bottle.

## Brushes

Nylon bristle brushes that come with children's paint sets are adequate for glue, but they are much too stiff for paint. Small cosmetics brushes with soft, natural bristles are perfect. If the only brushes available are too broad, trim them to a point with scissors.

## Pencil and Ruler

A pencil and a standard ruler come into play for most of the projects.

## Utility Knife

The utility knife is a useful tool for many of the beads in this book. It brings relief from the responsibility of rolling a cylinder bead with perfectly even ends. Any irregularities come off with a few strokes.

The carved projects in chapter six use a utility knife. One is optional for tapering the ends of many of the other beads. Paper dulls the blade rapidly, so have replacement blades on hand.

When using a utility knife, always cut with the blade facing away from the hand holding the bead. Don't cut with a back-and-forth sawing motion. Single, downward strokes are the most effective.

## Paints and Markers

Paint is featured in chapter four, and in parts of chapters two, six and seven. Any kind of paint will work. Expensive acrylics aren't necessary. I've had success with even the cheapest children's watercolor sets. I cover the cakes with water and let them sit for a while to thicken the paint.

Felt-tip markers are a good substitute for paint, as shown in some of the projects in chapter two. They're much easier than paint for beginners and youngsters.

## Other Materials

Chapter seven explores alternative materials, primarily cotton balls, fabric scraps and yarn.

## Specialty Supplies

A craft shop or other specialty store will have a far greater variety and higher quality of paints, markers, construction paper, tissue paper, yarn and fabric. It's worth while to pick up a couple of fine-tipped paint brushes. Another handy item is a single-edged razor. It will stay sharp longer than a utility knife blade. It makes a good tool for trimming plastic sticks.

A see-through quilter's ruler speeds along the process of measuring and marking the paper. I highly recommend purchasing one if you anticipate making a lot of beads. For making beads in quantity, a small can or bottle of varnish is much more economical than nail polish. Acrylic varnish is best, since it's less smelly and easier to clean up than enamel.

## Drying Racks

A bead in progress needs a place to rest between coats of paint and varnish. Drying racks can be as simple as a small glass or a lump of clay. A narrow box top, with notches to keep the beads from rolling against each other, is also handy. For plastic swabs and other hollow sticks, an efficient setup is a shallow box with pins pushed through from below. A dot of glue at the base of each pin prevents them from loosening. I favor this arrangement because it can be large enough to hold dozens of beads at a time, but still moved from place to place quickly and easily, without beads knocking against each other.

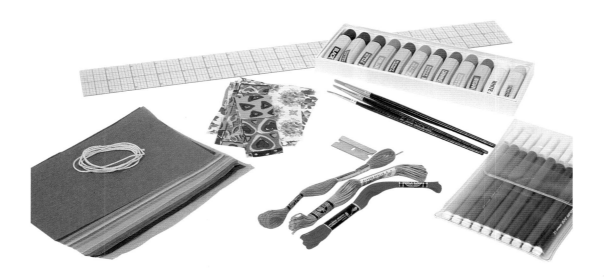

**Specialty Items** These specialty items are useful, but not absolutely necessary.

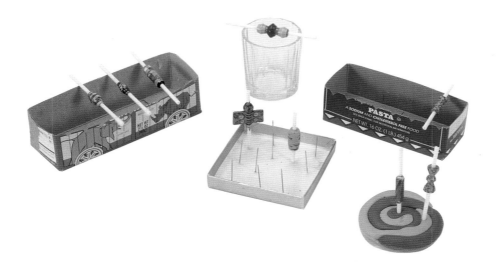

**Drying Racks** Paper beads don't require a forge, furnace or kiln. A drying rack, however, is essential.

## Bead Dimensions

The group of beads on this page shows how the diameter of the stick, the thickness of the paper and the length of the paper dramatically affect the shape of the bead.

Beads 1, 2 and 3 are made with identical strips of construction paper, each twelve inches (30.5cm) long. The only difference is the diameter of the stick. Bead 1 uses a plastic drinking straw, and bead 2 the same plastic swab used throughout this book. The needle used for bead 3 is the smallest stick and generates the most sharply defined shape.

Like bead 2, bead 4 is made of construction paper rolled on a plastic stick, but the strip of paper is only six inches (15.2cm) long. The shorter strip generates a decidedly less curvaceous shape.

Bead 5 uses a swab, and a twelve-inch (30.5cm) strip of paper. The difference is the thickness of the paper. The typing paper used in this bead is much thinner than construction paper, so it yields a more subtle shape.

## Finishing Touches

Nail polish and other varnishes will darken the bead. This sharpens some color contrasts, but it may obliterate others, so it's important to test the varnish on scraps of the materials before investing time in a complicated bead.

Be wary of using acrylic varnish on beads decorated with paint or markers. The varnish may smear and run them. It has a similar but less noticeable effect on colored tissue paper. When using these materials, seal the colors with an initial coat of enamel varnish, like nail polish, and save the acrylic for subsequent coats.

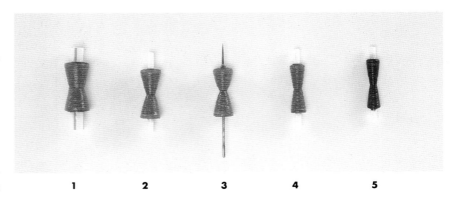

1    2    3    4    5

Experiment with different sticks and papers to get a feel for their effect on the dimensions of the bead.

Test the varnish to see how it darkens paper, paint or other materials, and to check for smearing and running. From left to right in the examples above notice that:
1. Acrylic varnish makes colored tissue run.
2. Nail polish holds the colors fast.
3. Varnish can intensify contrasts.
4. Varnish darkens fabric.
5. Varnish can erase contrasts.

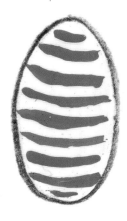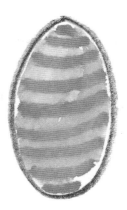

Use an enamel varnish, like nail polish, to seal water-based paints and markers. From left to right in the above examples notice that:

1. Acrylic smears watercolor paints.
2. Nail polish locks in the colors.
3. Acrylic washes out water-based markers.
4. Nail polish keeps the colors fast.

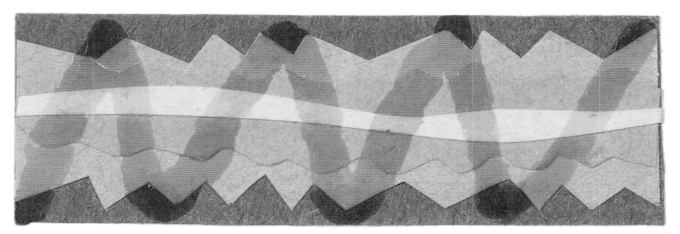

Varnish can darken paper significantly while intensifying its colors.

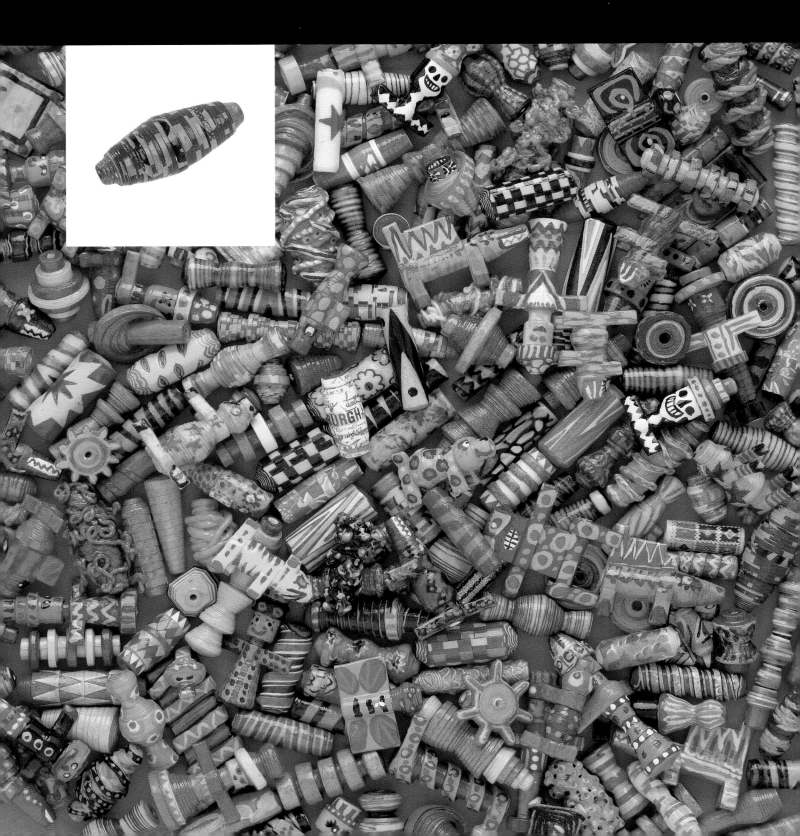

# CHAPTER TWO

# The Basic Bead

**A**ny colorful piece of paper has bead potential. This first project uses one of the most common types of paper known to modern civilization, headlines from advertisements in the Sunday newspaper.

Headlines from advertisements generate snappy looking beads because the letters and background form sharp contrasts.

Advertising headlines generate snappy looking beads because the letters and background form a progression of sharp contrasts. Keep this in mind when choosing paper. A photograph of a flower may look beautiful, but the slight transition between shades and colors will produce a bead with a more subtle pattern.

A long, slim triangle is the shape of the paper strip used for rolling a basic round bead. Without delving too deeply into the mysteries of geometry, this shape should be known by its proper name, the *isosceles triangle*. An isosceles triangle has two sides of equal length. Many of the beads in this book are based on isosceles triangles.

When cut from thin paper like newsprint, the isosceles triangle generates a slim, cigar-shaped bead. The bead gets a beefier, barrel shape with a foundation of construction paper. The foundation is a long rectangle of paper, which rolls up to form a cylinder. Cylinders also figure prominently in this book because most of the beads begin with a cylinder bead.

The following group of projects calls for scissors, glue, a small paintbrush to apply the glue (and a small dish to put it in), construction paper, clear nail polish, and plastic swabs or other slim sticks. Decorative paper, like advertising headlines or gift wrap, is also needed. A utility knife is optional.

## Steps for a Basic Round Bead

NOTE: Diagram is not proportional.

6"

¾"

**1 Cut Cylinder Base**
Cut a strip of construction paper ¾" (1.9cm) wide and 6" (15.2cm) long for the cylinder base.

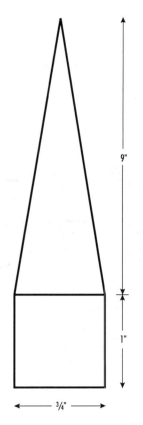

9"

1"

¾"

**2 Cut Triangle**
Cut a long isosceles triangle from any colorful piece of paper 9" (22.9cm) long and ¾" (1.9cm) wide at the bottom. The 1" (2.5cm) extension attached to the bottom in this diagram is optional. The extension makes the decorative paper cover the entire surface of the cylinder base.

# Basic Round Bead

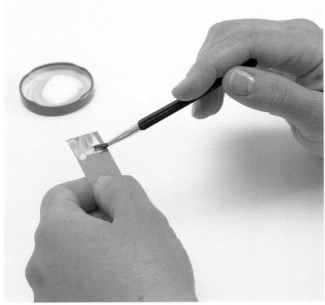

**3** **Glue Cylinder Base**
Brush a thin, even coat of glue on one end of the construction paper, covering about ½″ (1.3cm) of it.

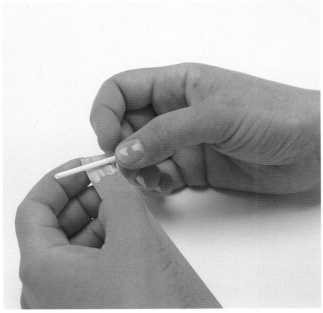

**4** **Begin to Roll Cylinder Base**
Position the stick on top of the glued section. Begin to roll the paper around the stick. If you have trouble getting started, try rolling the paper back and forth against the stick a few times. This will soften and curl the paper, making it easier to handle.

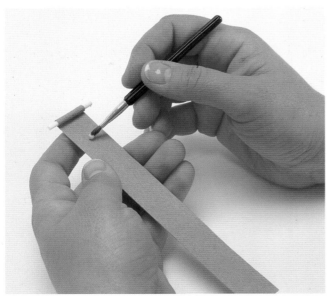

**5** **Roll and Glue**
Continue to roll the paper around the stick. Press down firmly with your thumbs to roll as tightly as possible. Add a few extra dots of glue as you go.

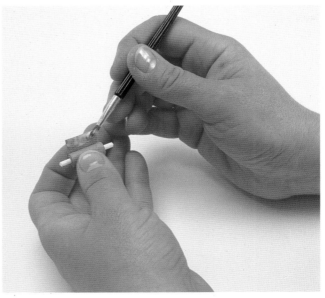

**6** **Glue and Press**
At the end of the strip, apply a thin, even coat of glue all the way across the top. Press it down and hold for a few seconds until the glue sets.

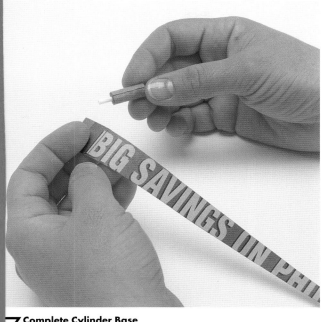

### 7 Complete Cylinder Base

This construction paper base is really a simple cylinder bead. It's the foundation for most of the beads in this book. You can do hundreds of things to it, but for now we'll just apply the decorative paper triangle.

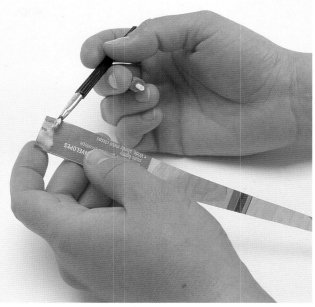

### 8 Glue Triangle

Apply a thin, even coat of glue covering about ½″ (1.3cm) of the extension on the triangle. If you have opted not to include the extension, just glue the first ½″ (1.3cm) of the triangle. Be sure to apply the glue to the wrong side of the paper.

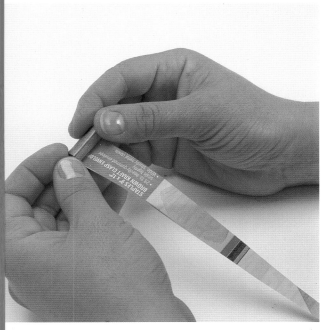

### 9 Position Triangle

Position the end of the extension evenly across the cylinder bead.

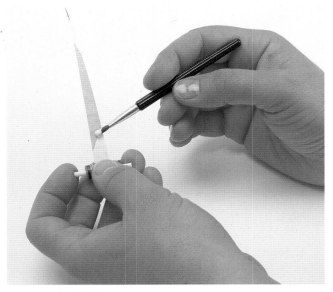

### 10 Roll and Glue

Start rolling the triangle around the cylinder. Keep the point of the triangle in the middle. Add a few extra dots of glue as needed.

# Basic Round Bead

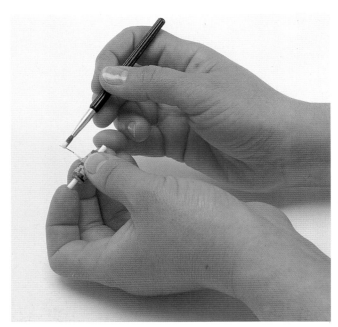

**11 Glue and Press**
At the tip of the triangle, brush on a thin coat of glue over the last ½″ (1.3cm) or so and press it down.

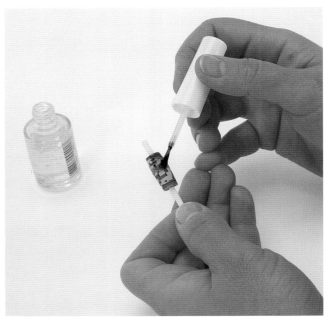

**12 Varnish**
The bead is essentially finished, but don't trim or remove the stick yet. It makes a convenient handle for holding the bead while brushing on the varnish. One coat of varnish is sufficient to waterproof the bead but because paper is so absorbent, two or three coats are needed for a high gloss. Wait several hours between each coat for the varnish to dry thoroughly.

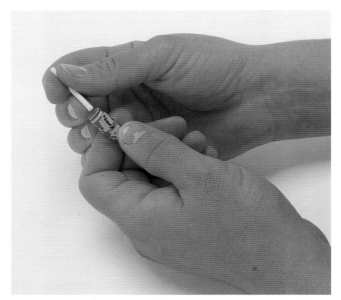

**13 Remove Stick**
After all the coats of polish are dry, grasp the bead in one hand and twist the stick with the other hand and pull it out. If it's stuck, don't try to force it out or the bead may come apart. Try gripping the stick with a pair of pliers and twisting until it turns freely, then pull.

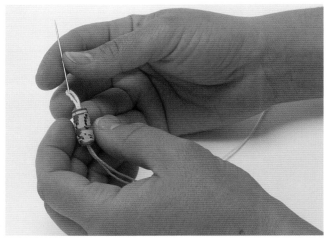

**14 Varnish Inside**
If you choose to remove the stick and the bead is expected to survive extreme weather conditions, waterproof the inside by soaking a piece of string in varnish and drawing it through the hole.

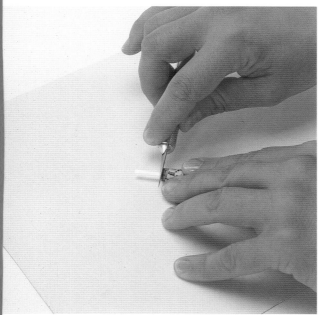

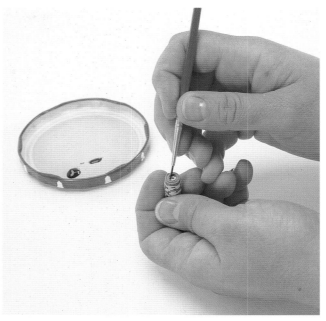

**15** **Trim Swab**
If you use a plastic stick or any hollow form, you can leave it inside the finished bead. Just trim it flush. Scissors will work, but a utility knife or razor produces a more precise edge. All of the beads in this book were finished with the swab left inside.

**16** **Paint Stick**
If you leave the stick inside and the light color doesn't contrast well with the rest of the bead, use paint to match it.

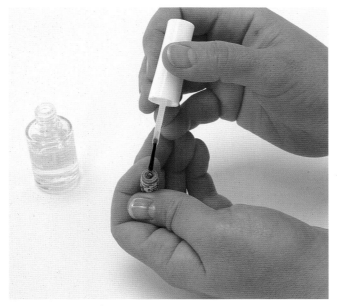

**17** **Varnish Ends**
To protect the paint and help secure the stick inside the bead, apply a bit of varnish to the ends.

# Basic Bead With Carved Ends

A quick way to jazz up a basic bead is to use two or more colors of construction paper for the cylinder base. Tapering the bead at both ends with a utility knife reveals the contrasting layers and creates a simple but attractive frame for the middle.

The base for the bead in this example is made with three different colors of construction paper, each ¾" (1.9cm) wide and 2" (5.1cm) long. The triangle of decorative paper is ½" (1.3cm) wide and 9" (22.9cm) long.

## Steps for a Basic Bead With Carved Ends

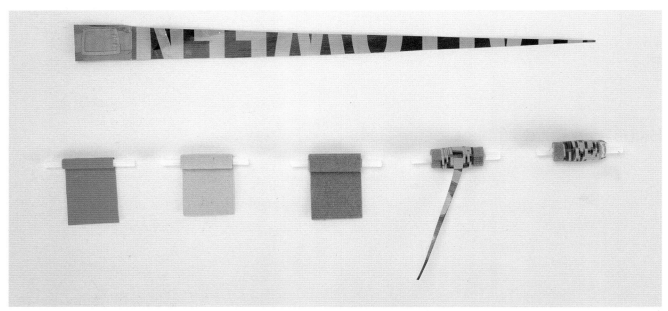

1. Cut a triangle of colored paper.
2. Roll the first piece of construction paper.
3. Add the second piece.
4. Add the third piece.
5. Add the triangle.
6. The completed bead before carving.

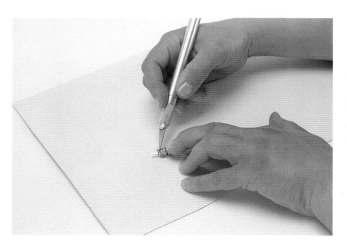

Carve the ends, angling the knife strokes to reveal the contrasting colors. Remember, when carving with a utility knife, always cut with the blade facing away from the hand that is holding the bead. Don't cut with a back-and-forth, sawing motion. Single, firm, downward strokes are the most effective.

# Tapered Base Bead

Even without a utility knife, you can achieve an attractively tapered shape by constructing the base from a tapered strip of paper. The delicate spirals at either end contribute an interesting aspect to the bead's overall design.

The shape of the paper strip for the tapered base is a *trapezoid*—nothing more than an isosceles triangle with its tip lopped off. The trapezoid becomes a familiar construction element in the chapters to come.

In this sample, the base is a trapezoid made of a 4″ (10.2cm) long strip of blue construction paper. As the diagram shows, the strip is tapered from a width of 1″ (2.5cm) at the bottom, to ¾″ (1.9cm) at the top. The rectangular extension upon which it sits lends extra thickness and strength to the ends of the bead. While rolling the tapered base, keep it centered so that both ends of the bead spiral inward evenly.

NOTE: Diagram is not proportional.

¾″

4″

1″

1″

**Diagram for a Tapered Base**

## Steps for a Bead With a Tapered Base

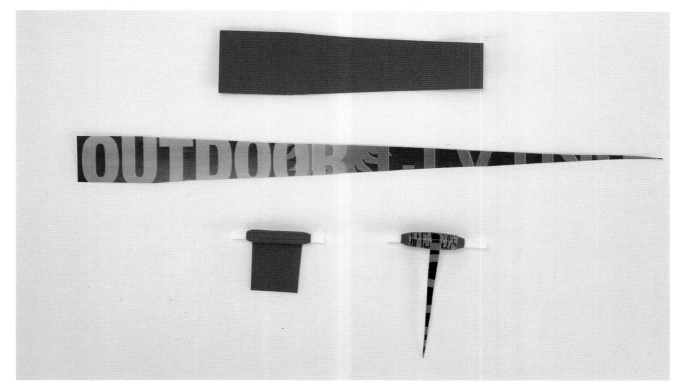

1. Cut a tapered base.
2. Cut a colored triangle.
3. Roll the base.
4. Add the triangle.

# Cylinder Bead

A cylinder base is a bead in its own right, only waiting for surface decoration to complete its transformation. One layer of paper with an especially intricate, colorful pattern will suffice.

In this sample, the base is a strip of construction paper ¾" (1.9cm) wide and 5" (12.7cm) long. Layered on top of the construction paper is a picture from a brochure advertising Oriental rugs. Other good sources for unusual, highly detailed designs are museum shop catalogs, pictures of linens and home furnishings, postage stamps and fine stationery.

## Steps for a Cylinder Bead

1. Cut a long strip of paper for the base.
2. Cut a short strip of paper for the applique.
3. Roll the base.
4. Add the applique.

# Just For Fun

Whether by definition or by habit, a bead possesses a hole so it can be strung on a string. However, once you've developed the skills to make paper beads, you can eliminate the middleman and make the bead directly into a piece of jewelry. Do this by rolling the strips of paper around a length of string, yarn, floss, leather, ribbon or chain.

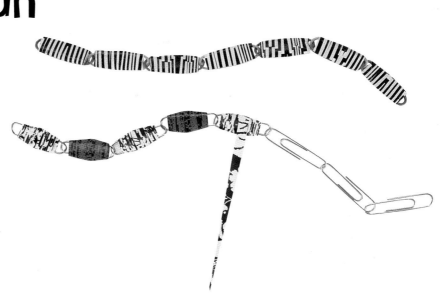

**Paper Clip Necklace** In this instant gratification sample, I roll basic round beads, made of contact paper, around a chain of linked paper clips. The contact paper has its own adhesive, saving a significant amount of time because no glue is required. Contact paper also eliminates the need to varnish the beads because it is waterproof and has its own glossy, durable finish. However, to be on the safe side, I do apply one quick coat to ensure that the tip of the triangle doesn't start to peel.

**Two-Step Necklace** A brightly colored elastic string is another convenient form upon which to make a necklace or bracelet. This sample starts with cylinder bases of black construction paper. Basic round beads, cut from a picture in an art catalog, are then layered on top. The bases are slightly wider than the triangles, so the black edges accent the colored middle.

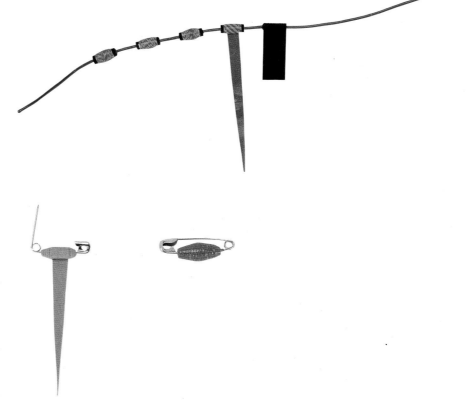

**Very Fast Brooches** Safety pins are fertile territory for the imagination. This subtle brooch is made by rolling a basic bead of purple construction paper directly around the back of a safety pin. The thick construction paper generates a much rounder shape than would newsprint or any other thin paper—a happenstance that we'll exploit to its fullest in the next few chapters. The distance between the two bars of the pin limits the circumference of the bead. If the bead is too big, the pin won't close.

# Custom Colors and Intricate Patterns

You'll need plain typing or photocopying paper and a set of markers or paints for the following group of projects.

At the risk of belaboring a point, any two-year-old can design paper that will generate an interesting bead. To produce the delicate looking bead pictured below, I cut my two-year-old loose on a cheap set of children's glitter paints that were too watery and tacky to be used for anything but stabbing violently with an old paint-brush onto a piece of plain typing paper.

Either markers or paints work with this technique. If you use paint, make the bead from a lightweight paper like ordinary typing or photocopying paper. On a heavy paper, like construction paper, the layers of dried paint will add more thickness and the resulting bead may appear awkward.

Hand-painted paper designed by a toddler, made into a bead by an adult.

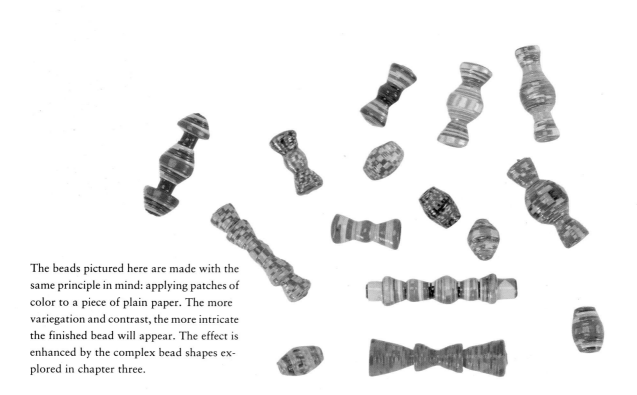

The beads pictured here are made with the same principle in mind: applying patches of color to a piece of plain paper. The more variegation and contrast, the more intricate the finished bead will appear. The effect is enhanced by the complex bead shapes explored in chapter three.

## Felt-tip Markers

Felt-tip markers are a convenient, easy-to-handle material for young artisans and other beginners. They can be used on light or heavy paper. They can, however, be unpredictable with regard to color loss over time. I've had excellent results with inexpensive sets, which I used for these samples but some of the colors in an expensive set of change-color markers vaporized the moment I varnished them.

In these samples, the triangles measure ½″ (1.3cm) wide by 8″ (20.3cm) tall, and they are sitting on a 4″ (10.2cm) extension. The edges of the extension are colored, so the ends of the finished beads will be colored instead of plain white.

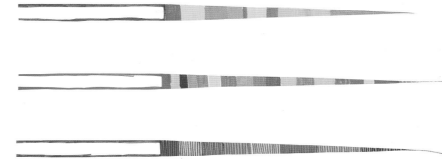

Changing colors frequently will produce a more extravagant bead. The top triangle emphasizes wide bands of color; the middle triangle narrow bands of color; and the bottom shows closely spaced lines drawn over wide bands of color.

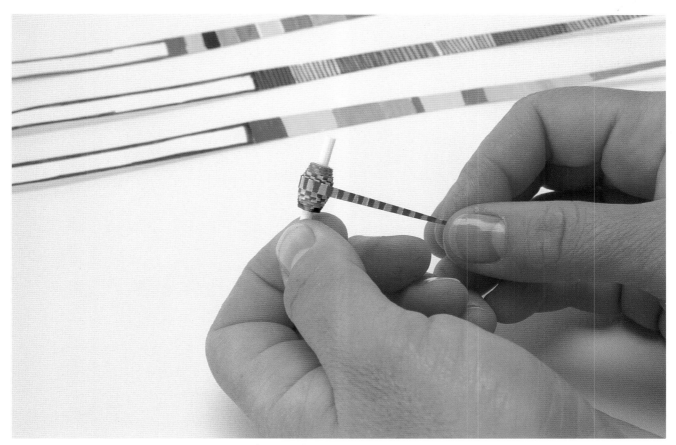

A variegated bead is one of many possible outcomes for hand-colored paper.

# Elegant Outlines

Another approach to hand-coloring, with a completely different effect, is constructing beads from very short triangles on very long extensions. In these beads, the triangle spirals around the bead only three times or so. A narrow outline of contrasting color—no more than ⅛″ (.3cm) in these samples—around the edge of the triangle creates the striped pattern.

Outlined beads work well when colored with markers. Use pale colored paper for the strongest contrast.

When outlining the paper, continue down the first inch (2.5cm) or so of the extension. This makes the line of color travel all the way around both ends of the finished bead.

NOTE: Diagram is not proportional.

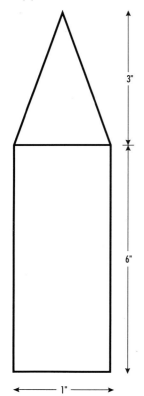

**Diagram for Outlined Bead**
The extension is 1″ (2.5cm) wide and 6″ (15.2cm) long and the triangle is 3″ (7.6cm) long.

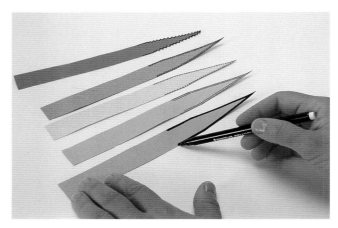

**Outlining the Shape**
The triangle itself may also be trimmed in a zigzag pattern, then outlined.

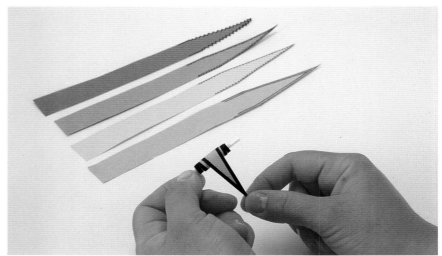

Roll the strip.

# Painted Outlines

To preserve a sleek, elegant profile, beads with painted outlines should be made of thin paper, like typing paper. Construction paper and other heavy paper will absorb a lot of paint, and the resulting bead may look cumbersome.

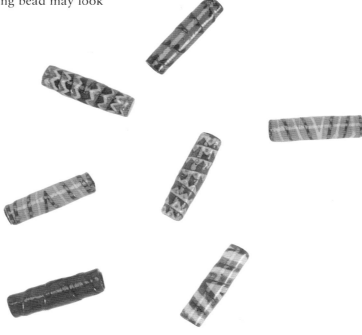

## Steps for a Painted Outlined Bead

1. Apply a base coat of color to white paper.
2. Make small triangles, no taller than ⅛″ (.3cm).
3. Fill in the triangles.
4. Dot each triangle.

# Colored Edges

This ethereal look is achieved by coloring the edge—not the surface—of the triangle. Use construction paper or some other heavy paper. This method works admirably on the complex shapes to be introduced in chapter three. But practice on a basic round bead first.

Paint and markers possess different advantages for the colored edge technique. Light colors of paint can be used to edge dark paper, an impossible feat for markers. But markers can take on a charmingly mysterious cast when the pigment bleeds slightly from the edge onto the surface of the paper. This is achieved by using water-based markers (not permanent markers), and brushing over the finished bead with water or with acrylic varnish to make the colors run. Normally, nail polish or some other enamel would be used, expressly to avoid such an occurrence.

## Steps for Bleeding the Colors of a Colored-Edge Bead

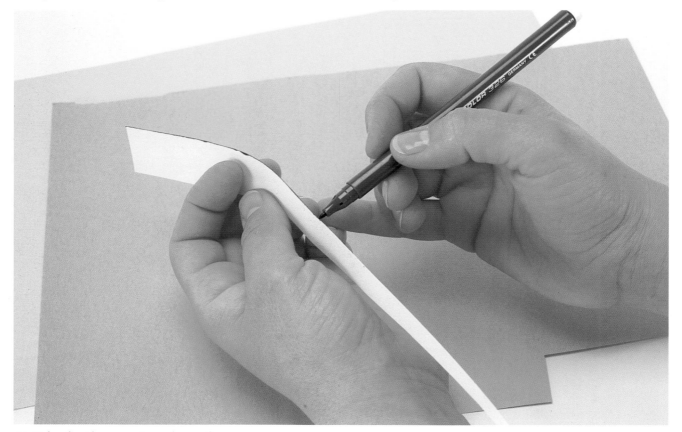

1 Color the edge—not the surface—of the paper with a marker. This maneuver is easiest when the paper is held up in the air.

**2** Roll the bead.

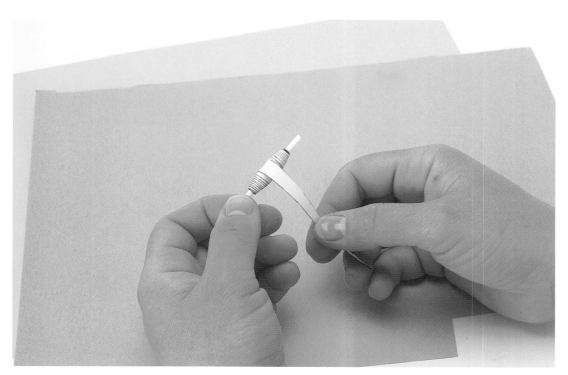

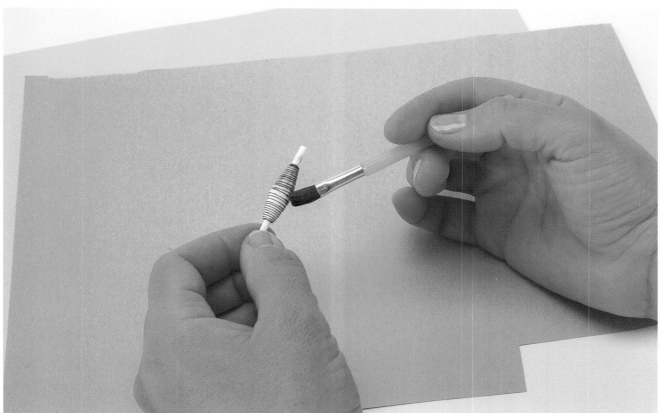

**3** Brush acrylic varnish firmly onto the bead to make the colors run. Go over each part of the bead several times if necessary. Or, brush the bead lightly with water.

# Flat Beads

With one strategic pinch we'll radically change the shape of a bead, making flat what was round. Like its cylindrical cousin, a flat bead is the springboard for innumerable variations. The simplest is to use it as a base for an applique. The flat surface is perfect for letters of the alphabet, photographs of people and other designs that would be lost on the round surface of a cylinder bead.

The flat bead is an important shape to master. You'll use it to make the elaborate creatures featured in chapter four.

The sample here uses a strip of construction paper ½″ (1.3cm) wide and approximately 12″ (30.5cm) long. The finished bead is ½″ (1.3cm) wide and ¾″ (1.9cm) long. I apply a small picture cut from a magazine over the finished bead. Find a suitable picture before deciding on the dimensions of your bead.

## Steps for a Flat Bead

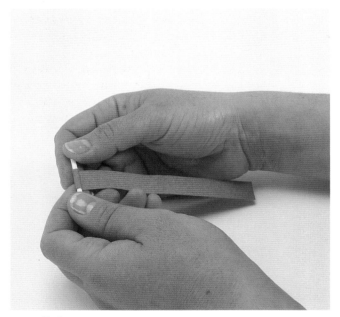

**1 Cylinder Base**
Glue and roll the strip of paper once or twice around a stick.

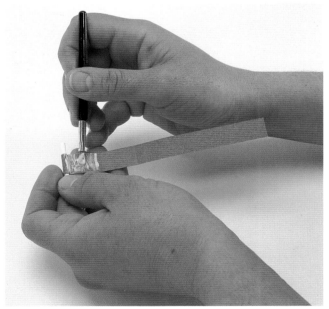

**2 Glue**
Apply a thin coat of glue over a section of the strip following the rolled part. This glued section should be as long as required to fit the applique you chose. In this sample, it's about ¾″ (1.9cm) long. Make sure to cover the entire surface of this section with glue. Work glue into the crevice between it and the rolled part.

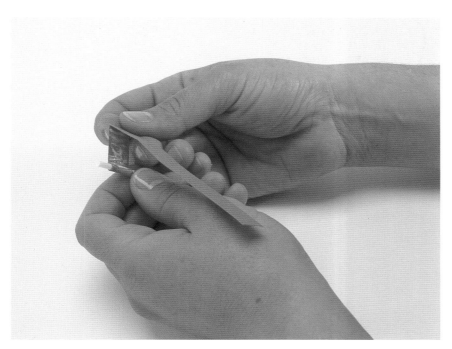

### 3 Fold

Fold the strip back toward the rolled section. The fold should be made exactly at the end of the glued section.

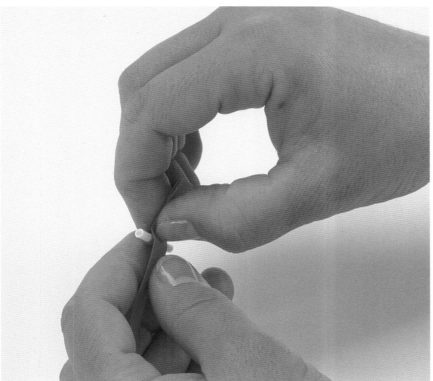

### 4 Press Firmly

Press the folded section firmly onto the glued section, eliminating any gaps between the two layers. If you haven't glued the entire surface, the layers will separate in places. If this happens, just peel them apart and apply more glue.

To get rid of the gap where the flat part of the bead meets the rolled part, pinch it between your thumbnails. If necessary, peel the strip back a little to apply more glue.

# Flat Bead

## 5 Glue Next Section

Brush glue onto the next section of the strip, approximately equal to the length of the bead.

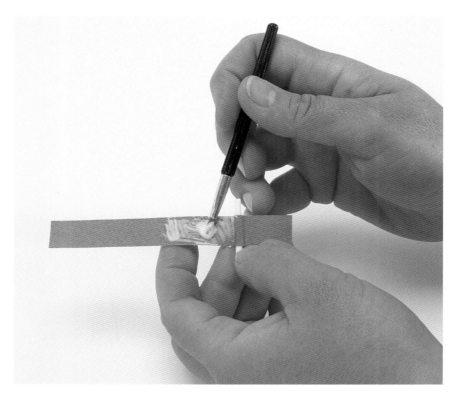

## 6 Continue to Glue and Fold

Now press this glued section around the rolled part of the bead, continuing onto the flat part. As in step four, pinch and crease the paper with your thumbnails to get rid of the gap between the two parts. Continue to glue the strip around the bead, one section at a time, until the flat part of the bead is thick and sturdy. Eight layers of construction paper will usually be sufficient.

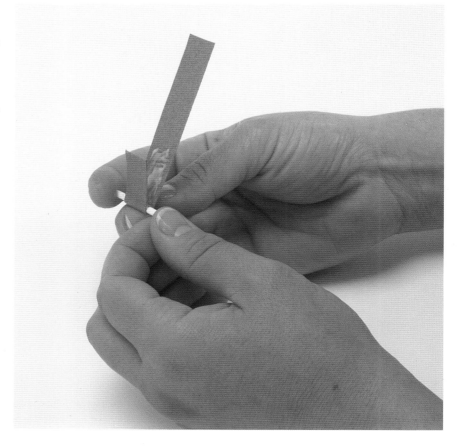

**7 Trim Picture**
Trim your picture to conform approximately to the bead.

**8 Final Trim and Glue**
Check the size of the picture against the bead before making a final trim. You can allow for a border around the picture, as in this sample, or make the picture long enough to cover both sides of the bead, as some of the other examples show. Glue the picture on the bead.

# Double Flat Bead

Insert another stick into the opposite end of a Flat Bead, and the result is a two-holed bead, which opens a whole new world of options for stringing and arranging beads. This method can be expanded to include three holes or even more.

## Steps for a Double Flat Bead

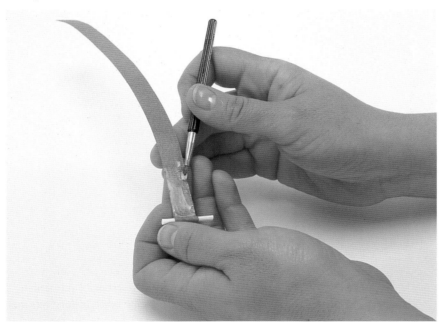

**1 Prepare First Stick**
Roll a ½" (1.3cm) wide by 12" (30.5cm) long strip of paper once or twice around a stick just like the cylinder base for the regular flat bead. Apply a thin coat of glue over the next 1" (2.5cm) or so of the strip, and onto the rolled part. Don't roll this glued section yet.

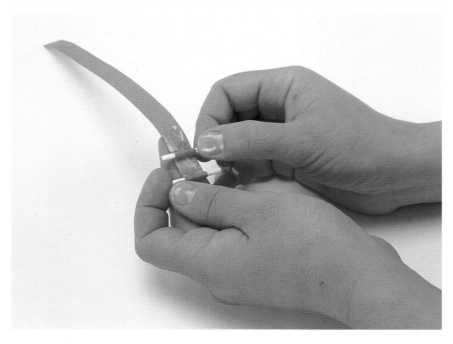

**2 Prepare Second Stick**
Roll a slim cylinder base ½" (1.3cm) wide by ¾" (1.9cm) long around a second stick. Then place the stick at the end of the previously glued section.

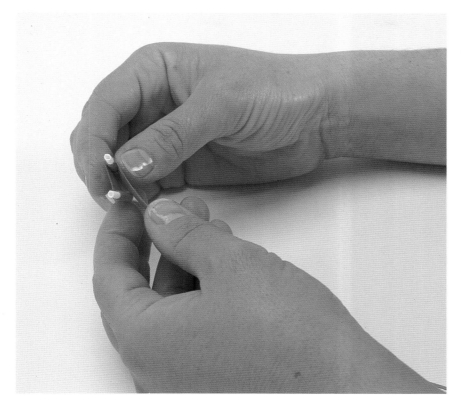

### 3 Roll and Press Second Stick
Roll the strip around the second stick and press it back toward the first stick.

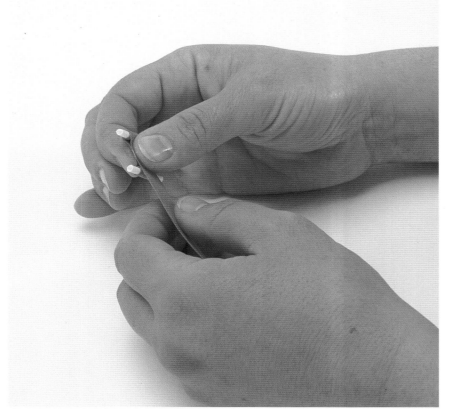

### 4 Continue Rolling and Pressing
Press the two sections of the strip firmly against each other, making sure they adhere completely. Pinch between your nails to eliminate the gap between the flat and cylinder parts at both ends of the bead. Continue rolling the strip around the bead, gluing the entire surface of the paper, until the flat part is about eight layers thick.

# CHAPTER THREE

# The Curvaceous Bead

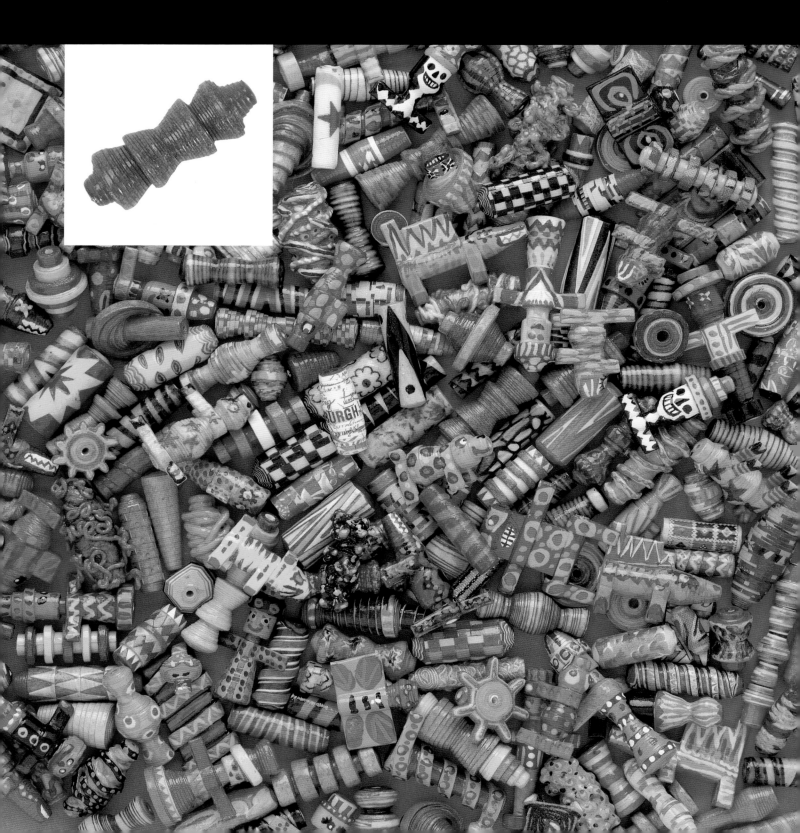

**N**ow it is time to delve into the essential character of paper. Measure, cut and roll a long, narrow strip of construction paper with exacting care and the resulting bead will possess a pronounced shape engraved with an intricate spiral. Bereft of any other surface decoration, this delicate pattern is intriguing enough to attract and hold the eye on its own. Therefore, I've resisted the temptation to slather paint over the beads made in this chapter. For now, we'll concentrate on shape, using only construction paper to enhance the design.

For a wider choice of colors, purchase packs of construction paper from two or more manufacturers. Many art stores sell construction paper by the sheet in a wide range of colors. Colored paper shopping bags are another alternative for achieving greater diversity.

## Right Triangle

Along with the isosceles triangle and the trapezoid, the other indispensable term in our bead vocabulary is the *right triangle*. Divide an isosceles triangle evenly in half, and the result is two right triangles. The distinguishing feature of a right triangle is the right angle in one of its corners. When the side with the right angle is rolled flush, it generates a cone shaped bead—exactly what you would get if you sliced a basic round bead down the middle.

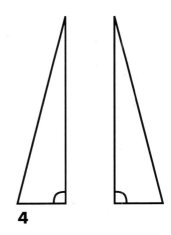

**3. Cut it in half . . .**

**1. An isosceles triangle . . .**

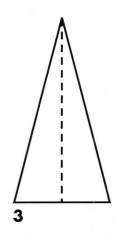

**4. . . . to get two right triangles . . .**

**2. . . . makes a round shape.**

**5. . . . and make two cone shapes.**

Different triangles make different bead shapes.

# Corset Bead

Two cone beads, tips together, make a corset shape. Exact measurements for the sample bead are provided in the diagram below. Duplicating this sample exactly is also a matter of using a plastic swab or other stick of the same diameter. Paper that is much thicker or thinner than the construction paper used here will create a bead with its own unique proportions.

Please notice that the diagrams are shorter and wider than actual size. In most of the diagrams in this book, the longest strip of paper measures no more than twelve inches (30.5cm). This is because the standard length of construction paper is twelve inches (30.5cm) and longer strips would have to be pieced together.

## Two Methods

There are two ways to approach the corset and other complex beads. Using one method, you can cut out the cylinder base and the different sections of the bead individually, and construct the bead one section at a time. This method is necessary when using different colors of paper and also serves well for practice, mass production and experiments with new shapes.

The second method is to cut a single strip of paper into a complex shape that incorporates all of the sections of the bead. I prefer this way, whenever the bead design allows, for the pleasure of transforming a single flat, featureless piece of paper into a three dimensional object. Another consideration is that all of the sections are attached and positioned in their proper order, which eliminates confusion.

The corset bead combines both methods. The cylinder base has three layers. The first two layers are two separate strips of paper, one red and the other yellow. The third layer is attached to the two triangles that make up the lavender corset section.

NOTE: Diagrams are not proportional.

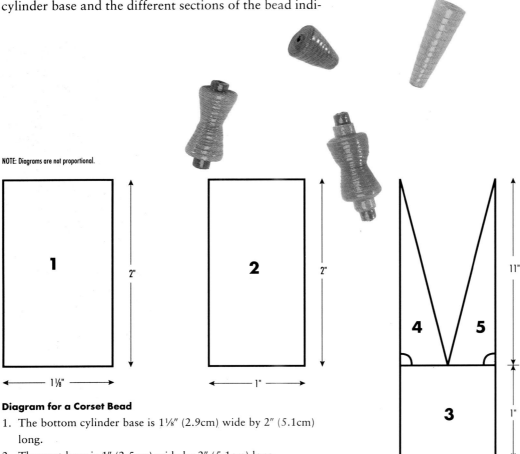

Please notice that the diagrams are shorter and wider than actual size to make it easier to see the geometric shapes and their relationships to each other.

**Diagram for a Corset Bead**

1. The bottom cylinder base is 1⅛″ (2.9cm) wide by 2″ (5.1cm) long.
2. The next base is 1″ (2.5cm) wide by 2″ (5.1cm) long.
3. The base of the corset shape is ¾″ (1.9cm) wide by 1″ (2.5cm) long.
4. Each right triangle is ⅜″ (1.0cm) wide by 11″ (27.9cm) long.
5. Same as above.

# Steps for a Corset Bead

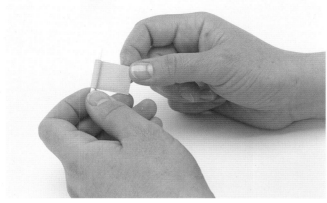

## 1 Cylinder Base
Roll a 1⅛" (2.9cm) wide by 2" (5.1cm) long strip of paper around a stick to make a slim cylinder base.

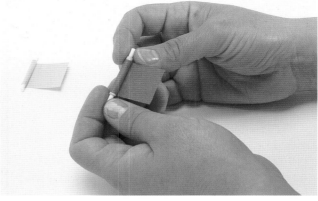

## 2 Layer Contrasting Color
On the top of the first base layer a 1" (2.5cm) wide by 2" (5.1cm) long strip of paper in a contrasting color. Center this strip so equal parts of the cylinder base are visible at either end.

## 3 Corset Strip
Add the corset strip. Glue the extension before rolling the two triangle sections.

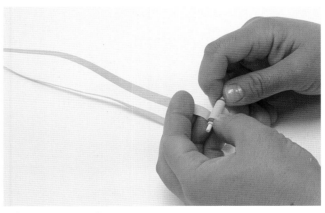

## 4 Roll One Triangle
Start rolling only one of the triangle sections. Rolling both at once is difficult. Allow the other triangle to flip around while you work on the first one. Keep the outer side flush, so it forms a straight edge. This will be the wide end of the cone shape. The inner side should begin to form a spiral.

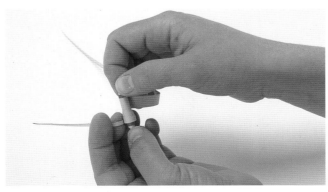

## 5 Roll Second Triangle
Continue rolling the triangle. Roll the second triangle in exactly the same manner.

# Bow Tie Bead

This versatile shape is one of my favorites, perhaps because my sweet tooth makes me swoon at the sight of this bead's candy-like silhouette. Two right triangles form the two outer cone shapes, and a slightly shorter isosceles triangle makes the inner basic round bead shape. Play with the width and length of all three triangles to discover the proportions that best suit your taste.

In this sample, the bow tie shape sits on a tapered base made of a trapezoid.

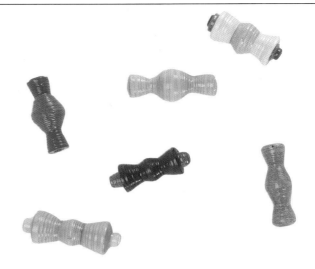

NOTE: Diagrams are not proportional.

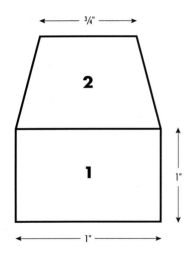

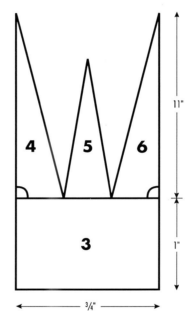

### Diagrams for a Bow Tie Shape

1. The extension for the trapezoid is 1″ (2.5cm) by 1″ (2.5cm).
2. The tapered base is a trapezoid, 1″ (2.5cm) wide at the bottom, ¾″ (1.9cm) wide at the top and 2″ (5.1cm) long.
3. The bow tie extension is ¾″ (1.9cm) wide by 1″ (2.5cm) long.
4. The two right triangles are ¼″ (.6cm) wide by 11″ (27.9cm) tall.
5. The isosceles triangle is ¼″ (.6cm) wide by 7″ (17.8cm) tall.
6. Same as 4 above.

### Steps for a Bow Tie Bead

1. Roll the trapezoid extension to make a slim cylinder base. Roll the trapezoid, making it spiral evenly on both sides.
2. Center the bow tie strip in the middle. Glue down the extension before rolling the triangles.
3. Roll one of the right triangles. Keep the outer edge flush to form the cone shape.
4. When rolling the inside triangle, keep its tip centered to form an even, round shape.
5. Roll the second right triangle, keeping the outer edge flush.

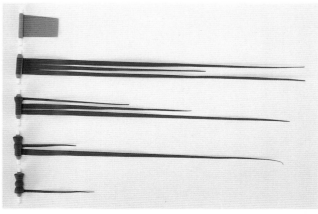

# Double Corset Bead

This shape lends itself well to mass production because all of the sections are identical right triangles. But, as with the bow tie bead, changing the width and length of the triangles produces an endless variety of new silhouettes.

In this sample, the cylinder base is flush with the ends of the double corset shape. The contrasting color provides a subtle accent, visible only if the bead is strung adjacent to seed beads or other small objects.

NOTE: Diagrams are not proportional.

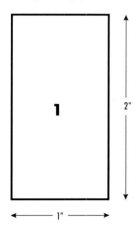

**Diagram for a Double Corset Bead**

1. The cylinder base is 1″ (2.5cm) wide by 2″ (5.1cm) long.
2. The extension for the double corset section is 1″ (2.5cm) by 1″ (2.5cm).
3. Each right triangle is ¼″ (.6cm) wide by 11″ (27.9cm) long.
4. Same as 3 above.
5. Same as 3 above.
6. Same as 3 above.

**Steps for a Double Corset Bead**

1. Make the cylinder base.
2. Add the double corset section. Glue down the extension before rolling the triangles.
3. Begin rolling one of the outside triangles, keeping the outer edge flush.
4. Work your way down the bead, going on to the second triangle . . .
5. and the third . . .
6. . . . and finally the fourth.

# Disc Bead

The disc shape is a narrow, many-layered cylinder bead. In these samples, it's only ⅛″ (.3cm) wide. Precision is the key to a good disc bead. To achieve—as near as humanly possible—flat surfaces on both sides, the long, narrow strips of paper must be cut perfectly straight. Scissors with long blades tend to work better than short blade scissors. A utility knife guided by the edge of a see-through ruler is a much better, and far quicker, method. This also eliminates pencil markings, which must be trimmed off or erased.

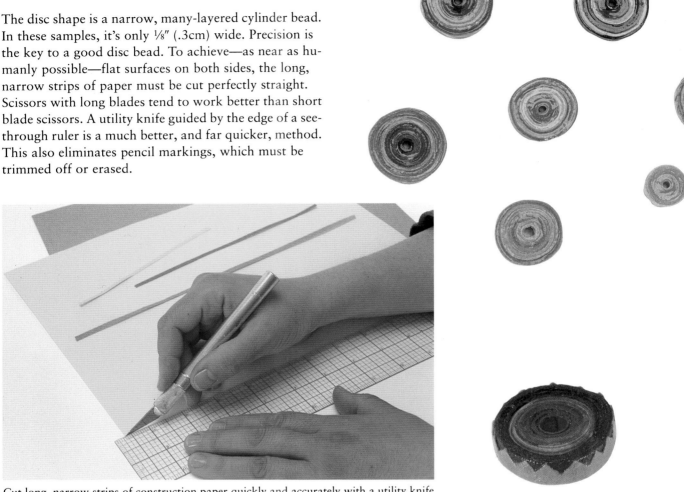

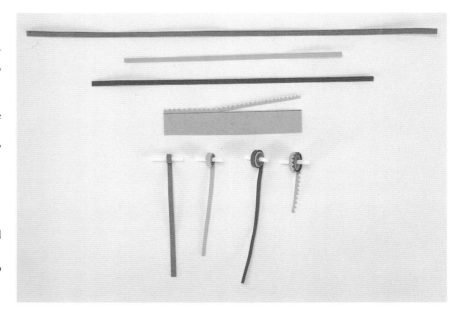

Cut long, narrow strips of construction paper quickly and accurately with a utility knife and a see-through ruler.

## Steps for a Disc Bead

1. Roll a ⅛″ (.3cm) wide by 12″ (30.5cm) long strip of paper around a stick. Rolling a disc is like rolling a cylinder bead, except more glue is needed to avoid shifting or unraveling. I coat the entire length of the strips with glue, to give the finished bead extra strength.

2. Add a contrasting ⅛″ (.3cm) wide by 6″ (15.2cm) long strip . . .

3. . . . then a ⅛″ (.3cm) wide by 8″ (20.3cm) long strip.

4. Finish with one layer of decorative paper or other trim. Here the trim is hand cut along one edge in zigzags. For ease of handling, measure the ⅛″ (.3cm) strip onto a wider piece of paper and cut it off after trimming the zig-zag.

# Saturn Bead

The defining feature of the Saturn is a disc bead layered onto a basic round bead. The disc section can be left as rolled or pushed askew to highlight the orbit-like effect.

The *planet* part of the Saturn is shaped by an isosceles triangle with the tip lopped off which geometrically speaking, isn't really a triangle, but a trapezoid.

When rolling the *orbit* part of the bead, glue each strip only at the beginning and the end so you can push it askew.

NOTE: Diagrams are not proportional.

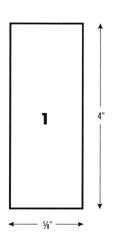

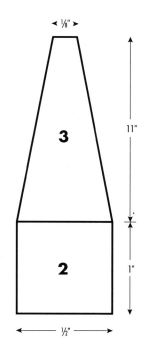

**Diagram for a Saturn Bead.**

1. The cylinder base is ⅝″ (1.6cm) wide by 4″ (10.2cm) long.
2. The extension on the trapezoid is ½″ (1.3cm) wide by 1″ (2.5cm) long.
3. The trapezoid is ½″ (1.3cm) wide at the bottom and ⅛″ (.3cm) wide at the top by 11″ (27.9cm) long.

**Steps for a Saturn Bead**

1. Roll the cylinder base.
2. Add the trapezoid shape in the middle of the cylinder base. Keep the tip centered so that both sides form an even spiral.
3. Layer on a disc bead made of two ⅛″ (.3cm) by 12″ (30.5cm) strips.
4. Same as 3 above.
5. This shows the finished bead, with the disc section left straight.

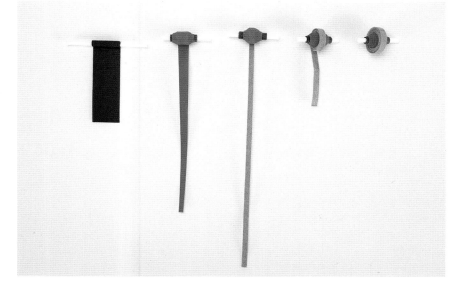

# Flower Bead

It appears complicated, but the flower is only a series of narrow flat beads arranged around a disc bead. If you skimmed chapter two without trying a flat bead, revisit it for practice.

The flower beads here are made of ⅛″ (.3cm) wide strips of construction paper. Cutting and measuring the narrow bits of paper accurately is the key to a neatly turned out bead. The entire surface of the strip must be glued, one small section at a time, for the bead to hold its shape.

## Steps for a Flower Bead

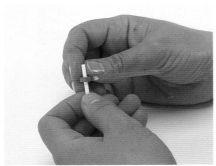

**1 Make Disc Bead**
Make a small disc bead from a single ⅛″ (.3cm) by 12″ (30.5cm) strip of paper. Glue as you roll.

**2 Glue To Start First Petal**
Attach another ⅛″ (.3cm) by 12″ (30.5cm) strip of a contrasting color. Start the first petal like a single flat bead by covering a short section of the strip with glue. The glued section here is ¼″ (.6cm) long. Work the glue into the crevice between the strip and the disc.

**3 Fold To Form First Petal**
Form the first petal by folding the strip at the end of the glued section back toward the disc.

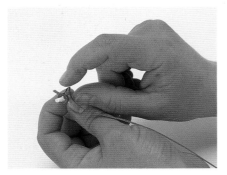

**4 Finish, Glue and Start More Petals**
Pinch the strip to eliminate gaps between the petal and disc. This completes the first layer of the first petal. Glue down the strip and start another petal. A scant ¼″ (.6cm) between petals should provide room for five or six on the flower.

**5 Add Layers**
After making all the petals, continue gluing the strip around the whole flower, adding more strips of paper when necessary. Make each petal about eight layers thick. A new color can be added at any point.

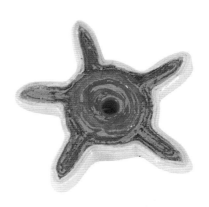

# Pendant Bead

So far all the beads in this book have been designed with a lateral hole, making the bead hang sideways when put on a string. Any bead can be made perpendicular, allowing it to hang down pendant-style from a necklace.

Instead of forming the pendant bead around a stick, first make a long, narrow flat bead. The sections of the bead will be rolled around the flat bead, treating it as a stick. Or . . . form the bead directly around a few strands of wire, with one end twisted into a loop for stringing.

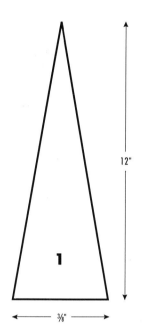
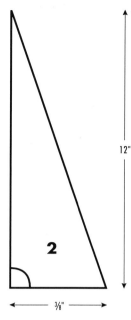

NOTE: Diagrams are not proportional.

**Diagram for a Pendant Bead**

1. The "head" is an isosceles triangle, ⅜″ (1.0cm) wide by 12″ (30.5cm) long.
2. The "skirt" is a right triangle, ⅜″ (1.0cm) wide by 12″ (30.5cm) long.

**Steps for a Pendant Bead**

1. Make a long, narrow flat bead from a ⅛″ (.3cm) by 12″ (30.5cm) strip of paper. The flat part of this bead is 1″ (2.5cm) long.
2. Add an isosceles triangle to make a head.
3. Using a ⅛″ (.3cm) by 12″ (30.5cm) strip of paper, make two flat beads for arms with the same technique used to make the petals on the flower bead.
4. Finish with a right triangle to make a skirt. Glue the triangle on with the right angle pointing down, so the base of the cone becomes the bottom edge of the skirt.
5. Using a ⅛″ (.3cm) by 6″ (15.2cm) strip of paper, layer on a disc bead to embellish the bottom of the skirt.

# CHAPTER FOUR

# The Bodacious Bead

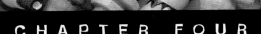

**C**onstruction paper, the workhorse of the paper bead craft, is the ideal for the vivaciously sculpted figures in this chapter. Thick and pliable, it supplies the heft and ease of handling needed to build complex shapes, and its surface readily absorbs paint. Brown grocery bags are another source for heavy, absorbent paper; the color of the paper is of no consequence because the entire surface will be painted. A set of paints and small brushes are also required for these projects.

## A Word About Painting

All painters, even those who still wear feetie pajamas, have their own distinctive style. Mine is of the Morse code school. No matter how involved my designs appear, they reduce to little more than a series of dots and dashes.

There are whole books on color theory, but in the Morse code school one rule suffices: When in doubt, go for contrast. The colors should stand out as distinct entities, instantly signaling to even a casual observer how much effort went into the creation. If you can't decide on a combination of colors, look around for objects that please your eye—a favorite shirt, a candy wrapper, a coffee mug—and use them as models.

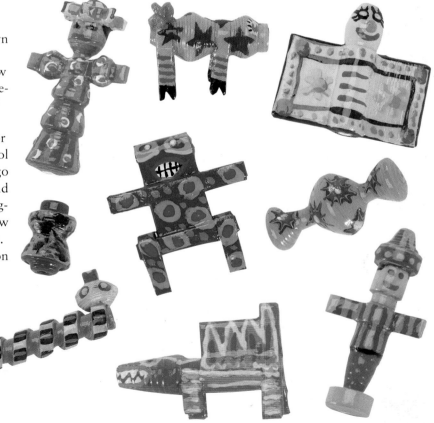

# Dots and Dashes

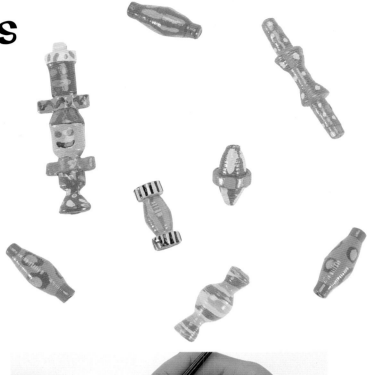

The surface of a construction paper bead is already distinguished by a delicate spiral pattern, so even a few crude strokes of the brush will be interesting. Also boosting the ooh-ah factor is a shape that's more complex than a basic round bead.

Any kind of paint can be used. Little jars of acrylic are the easiest to handle, but a wide selection of colors can be expensive. The paint used for these beads was an inexpensive set of liquid watercolors. Packaged in small tubes, the paint is thick enough to use as is. Thicken watercolors that come in dry cakes by covering the surface of each cake with water, waiting a few minutes to let it absorb, and then mixing it thoroughly with a brush. If the paint is too thin, the pigments run and feather out.

## Steps for a Simple Design

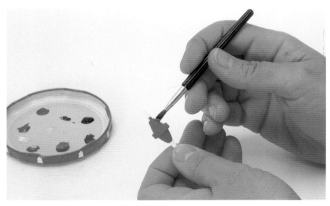

**1 Cover with Base Color**
Cover the surface of the bead with a base color. This smooths the bumps of the spiral somewhat without erasing the pattern entirely.

**2 Highlight Sections**
Highlight the different sections of the bead with a contrasting color. Here, blue sets off the middle from the ends.

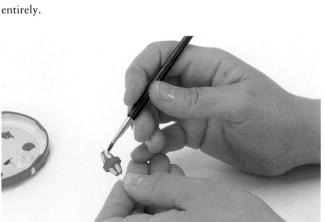

**3 Stripe the Ends**
Use another contrasting color to stripe the ends.

**4 Dot the Middle**
With a fourth color, dot the middle.

The sample bead is the Saturn shape (see chapter three), but with a smaller orbit.

# Complex Designs

The more patience applied to a project, and the smaller the paintbrush, the more fascinating the result. Paint these beads with the same Morse code method used in the simple design, except don't stop after a few dots and dashes.

Because these decorations are intricate, they transform even a basic round bead into an object of great interest. A complicated silhouette like the Double Corset (see chapter three) in the following sample only heightens the intrigue.

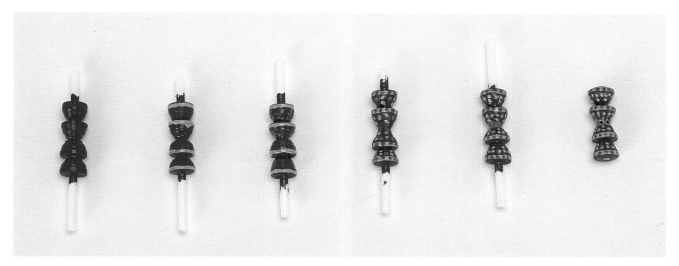

### Steps for a Complex Design

1. Apply a base color over the entire surface.
2. Highlight the different sections. Here it's done with a stripe of yellow around the wide edge of each cone.
3. Make several stripes across the middle of each cone.
4. Put dots on top of and in between all the stripes.
5. Accent the middle of the bead with a contrasting stripe and, where possible, layer dots on top of some of the other dots.
6. On the band at the bead's center add two layers of dots.

# Special Effects

The success of the dot and dash method relies on having enough patience to wait for one layer of paint to dry before applying the next. Impatience, however, can be exploited to obtain a vastly different effect. For the results shown here, paint as fast as possible, splashing color on color while still wet.

## Marbleizing a Bead

This is a quick way to decorate a bead, just a few strokes cover the bead with captivating swirls of color. Coat the entire bead with a heavy base color, dotting it with a contrasting color. Then swirl the two colors around with a toothpick. Tend to the paint like a hothouse flower. It must be thin enough to allow the colors to entwine each other, but thick enough to prevent them from becoming undistinguishable.

**Steps for Marbleizing**

1. Cover the surface of the bead heavily with a base color.
2. While the base coat is still wet, dot it with a contrasting color.
3. Draw a toothpick lightly through the dots and base coat to make the two colors swirl around each other.

## Faux Millefiori Bead

The look of colored glass beads also requires paint thin enough to run a bit, but not so thin that the colors feather into each other.

Work quickly, while the paint is wet. It helps to use a different brush for every color, eliminating the time needed to clean the brush between colors. Doing one flower at a time, as illustrated here, also helps ensure that the process is complete before the paint dries.

For dots as thick and wet as possible, it's helpful to scrape the drops of paint from the brush with a toothpick. The alternatives—shaking the brush or touching it to the paper—are less effective.

## Primitive Bead

This distinctive textured look is achieved by coating the bead with a thick layer of colored glue rather than paint. While the glue is wet, scratch a simple design with a toothpick or a blunt nail. To color the glue, pour a spoonful of plain white glue into a small dish. Add a bit of paint, a drop at a time, until you have a deep, rich color.

Scratching with a toothpick reveals the paper underneath the layer of glue-thickened paint. Choose a paint that contrasts strongly with the color of the paper for dramatic results.

You can achieve contrasts between two paints by covering the bead with a base coat of paint, letting it dry, and then layering it with the colored glue. Use a lighter touch to scratch the design to reveal the base color but not the paper.

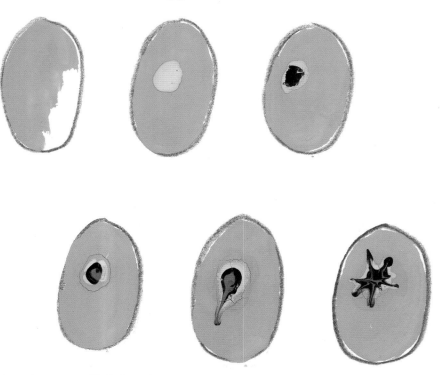

**Steps for a Faux Millefiori Bead**

1. Paint the surface of the bead with a base color.
2. While the base color is still wet, put a dot of contrasting paint on it.
3. Layer on another dot . . .
4. . . . and a third dot.
5. Draw a toothpick lightly from the center of the dots to the outer edge.
6. Repeat step five all around the dot, wiping the toothpick clean after each stroke.

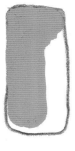   

**Steps for a Primitive Design**

1. Apply a base coat of normal paint to the bead. Let it dry before proceeding to the next step.
2. Coat the bead with a thick layer of colored glue.
3. With a toothpick, scratch a design onto the bead. Keep it simple enough to complete the entire bead before the glue/paint mixture dries.
4. As long as the glue/paint mixture stays wet, add more detail.

# Butterfly Bead

To make the remaining beads in this chapter, you must be familiar with the geometric shapes described in chapters two and three: isosceles triangle, right triangle and trapezoid. You should also be on friendly terms with the Flat bead from chapter two.

As in chapter three, all the diagrams are much shorter and wider than actual size, so the geometric shapes and their relationships to each other are easier to visualize. Transpose the diagrams by eye or use the exact measurements to make a precise copy of the sample bead.

The instructions for the butterfly show the bead being constructed from three separate pieces of paper—a rectangle for the cylinder base, an isosceles triangle for the head and a long strip for the flat wings. The butterfly and most of the other beads in this chapter can be constructed from a single piece of paper, just like the complex beads in chapter three, by leaving the base section attached to the other elements of the shape.

I prefer the all-of-one-piece method. I like getting the brain work—measuring, cutting and arranging—for a quantity of beads out of the way. Then I can sit down with a stack of papers and roll them with all the elements already attached to the base section in their proper order on a single strip of paper.

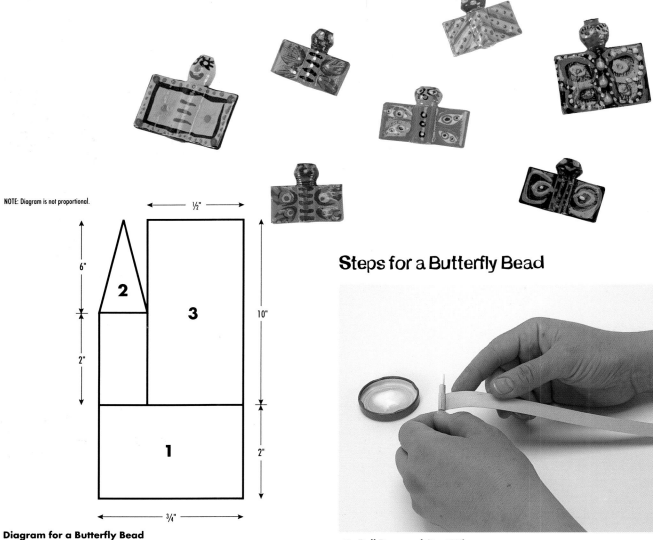

**NOTE:** Diagram is not proportional.

## Steps for a Butterfly Bead

### Diagram for a Butterfly Bead

1. *Base.* The base is ¾" (1.9cm) wide by 2" (5.1cm) long.
2. *Head.* The head is an isosceles triangle ¼" (.6cm) wide by 6" (15.2cm) long, sitting on a 2" (5.1cm) long extension.
3. *Wings.* The wings are a ½" (1.3) wide by 10" (25.4cm) long strip.

### 1 Roll Base and Start Wings

First roll the base section to make a slim cylinder bead. Then glue the long strip to the cylinder base to start the wings. Keep one side of the strip flush with one end of the cylinder. Roll it about halfway around or just enough to attach it.

**2 Start First Wing**
Make a flat bead from the long strip to form the first wing. Coat the first ½″ (1.3m) of the strip with glue, and work glue into the crevice between the strip and the cylinder.

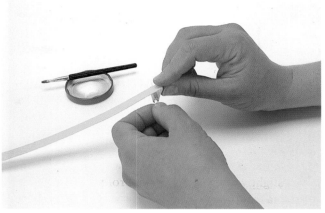

**3 Complete First Wing**
Begin where the glued section ends and fold the strip back toward the base to make a ½″ (1.3cm) long wing. Eliminate the gap that occurs between the wing and the cylinder section by pinching the gap between your nails.

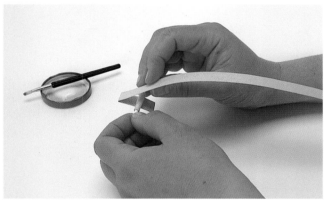

**4 Second Wing**
To start the second wing, continue to glue the strip around to the opposite side of the cylinder. Then coat ½″ (1.3cm) of the strip with glue, and fold it back as in step three. Continue to fold the strip around both wings, gluing thoroughly, until each wing is at least eight layers thick.

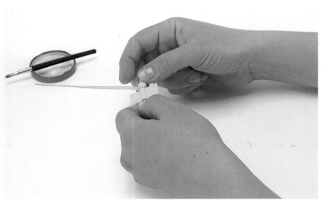

**5 Head**
Roll the small triangle to make the head.

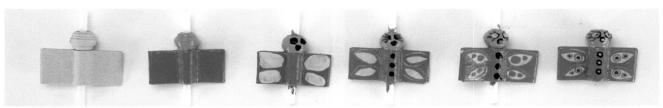

**Steps for Painting a Butterfly Bead**

1. The completed butterfly.
2. Assign a different color to each section.
3. Three black dots make two eyes and the mouth. Four yellow ovals make four wings. A few narrow stripes add interest to the body.

4. Use a very fine tipped brush for the following steps. Outline the wings with a contrasting color. Paint small lines for eyelashes. Dot a row of buttons onto the middle of the body.

5. Put two dots inside each wing, one in each eye, and one in the mouth.
6. Fit a tiny dot in the eyes and buttons. On top of each dot in the wings, layer two more dots.

# The Head Bead

These heads include shoulders, so they'll face in the right direction when strung on necklaces or bracelets. Without the shoulders, they spin around and always seem to wind up with their backs to the audience. The extravagant hats are based on the bead shapes from chapter three. Instructions for them are on pages 58 and 59.

As the diagram indicates, the hat, head and chin sections for the sample bead form a trapezoid. The trapezoid is slightly lopsided, and I've broken it into sections just to make it clear that one side is angled more sharply than the other. This diagram makes a long spiral for the hat crown and a short, very tight spiral for the chin. A stumpy hat and a droopy chin are not as appealing.

The brim of the hat is made from a separate strip of paper.

Painting a face is purely a matter of personal taste. It can be as simple as two dots for the eyes and a dash for the mouth. My skeleton heads are just a bit more complicated than that.

**Diagram for a Head Bead**

1. *Base.* The base is 1" (2.5cm) wide by 1½" (3.8cm) long.
2. *Hat Crown, Head and Chin.* The hat crown, head, and chin are a trapezoid, ¾" (1.9cm) wide at the bottom, ⅜" (1.0cm) wide at the top and 8½" (21.6cm) long.
3. *Neck.* The neck is an empty space on the base, ⅛" (.3cm) wide.
4. *Shoulders.* The shoulders are a strip ⅛" (.3cm) wide by 10½" (26.7cm) long.

NOTE: Diagram is not proportional.

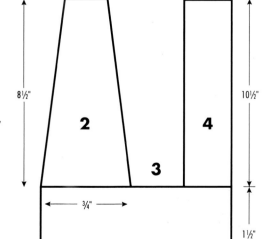

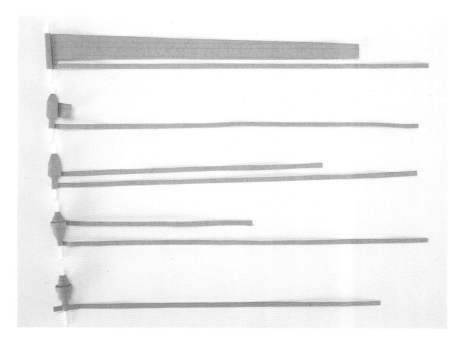

**Steps for a Head Bead**

1. Roll the base onto the stick.
2. Roll the head/hat/chin section, keeping the chin attractively short.
3. Position a separate ⅛" (.3cm) wide by 8" (20.3cm) long strip of paper on the head section just below the crown.
4. Roll the strip around the head five or six times to form the brim of the hat.
5. Glue and pinch two flat beads for the shoulders.

**Steps for Painting a Skull**

1. Coat the entire bead with white paint.
2. Make two dots for the eyes and a triangle for the nose. Outline a sideways crescent for the mouth.
3. Make lines for the teeth.
4. Outline the face in black.
5. Fill in with black the entire outlined area behind the face.
6. Make a black zigzag all around the neck and shoulders.
7. Fill in the outer edge of the zigzag with black.

### Flowers for a Hat

1. Cover the bead with a base coat. For the brim, paint a slim line in another color.
2. Make small and large dots randomly around the hat.
3. Make an "X" in the middle of each large dot.
4. Make a dot in the middle of each "X."

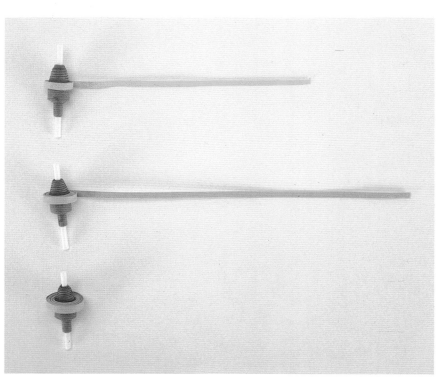

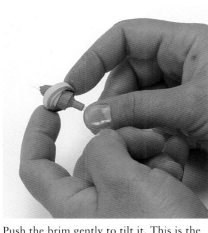

Push the brim gently to tilt it. This is the same maneuver used for the Saturn bead in chapter three.

### Steps for a Sombrero

1. Make the basic head shape, using a ⅛″ (.3cm) by 12″ (30.5cm) strip of paper for the brim. Glue only the beginning and end of the strip.
2. Layer another ⅛ (.3cm) by 12 (30.5cm) strip on the brim.
3. The finished brim, before pushing it to tilt.

**Diagram for a Tiered Hat**

1. *Base.* The base is 1″ (2.5cm) wide by 1½ (3.8cm) long.
2. *Top Tier.* The top tier of the hat is ⅛″ (.3cm) wide by 3½″ (8.9cm) long.
3. *Middle Tier.* The middle tier of the hat, along with the head and chin, is a lop-sided trapezoid, ⅝″ (1.5cm) wide at the bottom, ½″ (1.3cm) wide at the top and 10½″ (26.7cm) long.
4. *Neck.* The neck is an empty space on the cylinder ¼″ (.6cm) wide. The shoulders have been left off this diagram.

NOTE: Diagram is not proportional.

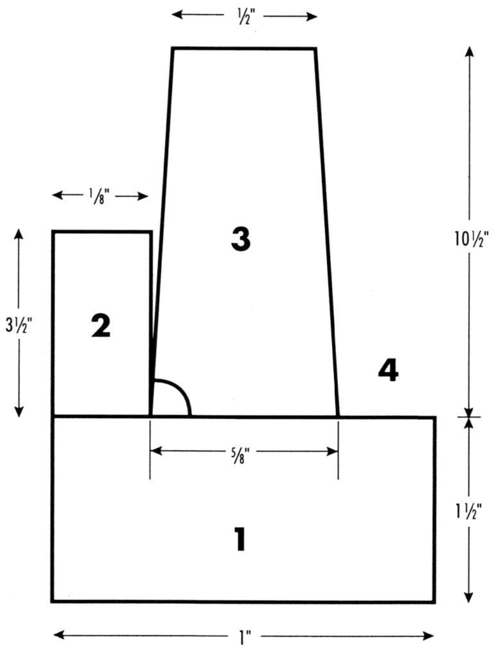


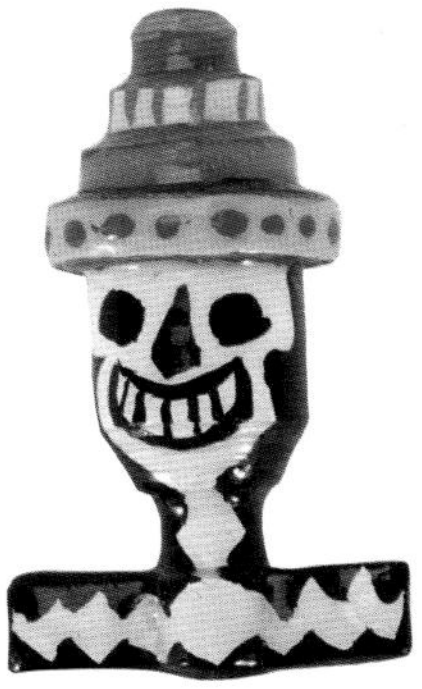

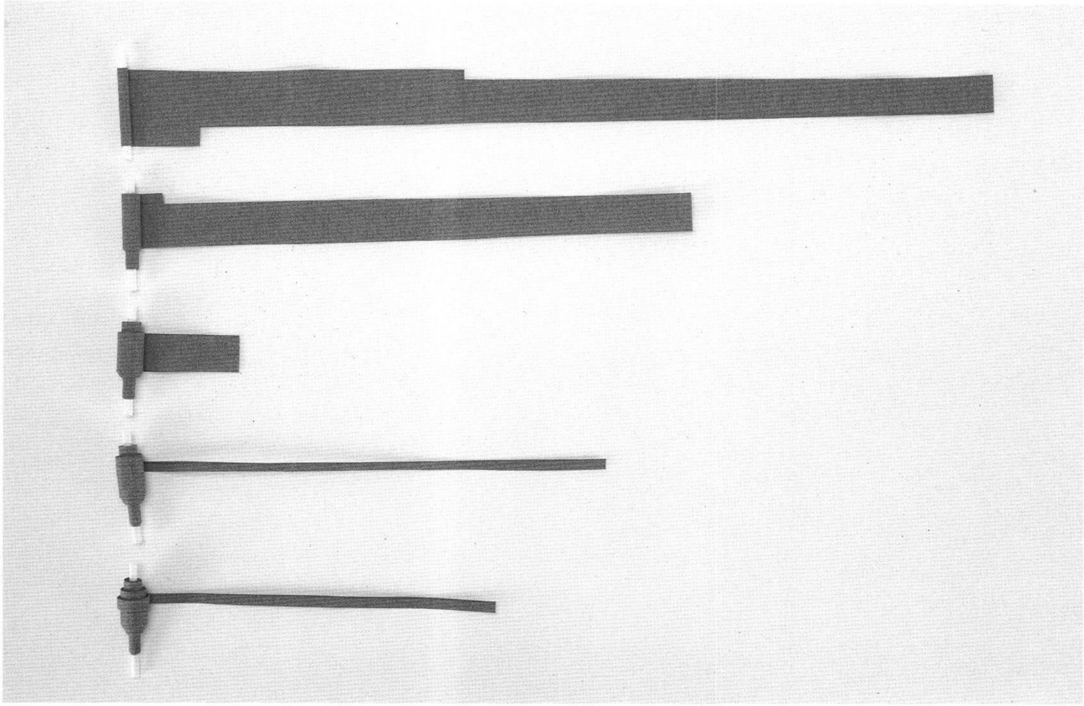

**Steps for a Tiered Hat**

1. Roll the base onto the stick.
2. Start rolling the hat/head/chin unit, keeping the top edge flush to form the top tier. When you reach the "step," glue it down.
3. Continue rolling the trapezoid to make the middle tier and chin.
4. Attach an extra strip of paper about ⅛″ (.3cm) below the middle tier.
5. Roll the strip to form the lower tier.

# A Man Bead

This is a fairly complicated figure. The head and hat together are similar to the three-tiered hat in the previous project except it has only two tiers, one for the crown and the other for the brim. A long, narrow cone forms the legs and a small disc serves as feet.

In addition to rearrangement of his hat, this man is amenable to change, like adding a torso or feet.

NOTE: Diagram is not proportional.

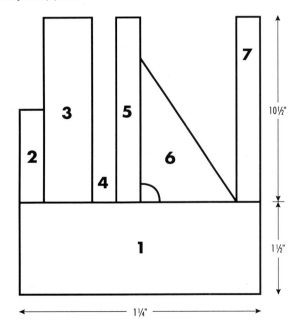

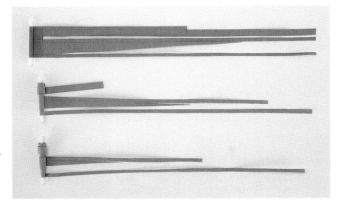

## Diagram for a Man Bead

1. *Base*. The base is 1¼″ (3.2cm) wide by 1½″ (3.8cm) long.
2. *Hat Crown*. The hat crown is ⅛″ (.3cm) wide by 5½″ (14cm) long.
3. *Head*. The head is ¼″ (.6cm) wide by 10½″ (26.7cm) long. A separate ⅛″ (.3cm) by 6″ (15.2cm) strip is added for the brim.
4. *Neck*. The neck is a ⅛″ (.3cm) wide empty space.
5. *Arms*. The arms are ⅛″ (.3cm) wide by 10½″ (26.7cm) long.
6. *Legs*. The legs are a right triangle, ½″ (1.3cm) wide by 8″ (20.3cm) long that can be cut and rolled in a unit with the arms, except for the top 3″ (7.6cm).
7. *Feet*. The feet are ⅛″ (.3cm) wide by 10½″ (26.7cm) long.

## Steps for a Man Bead

1. Roll the base onto a stick.
2. Roll the hat/head unit (the brim will be added later).
3. Roll the arms/legs unit. The legs start forming a cone, tip down. Stop rolling when there is 6″ (15.2cm) left to the arms section. If you haven't already, cut the remaining 3″ (7.6cm) of the legs free from the arms.

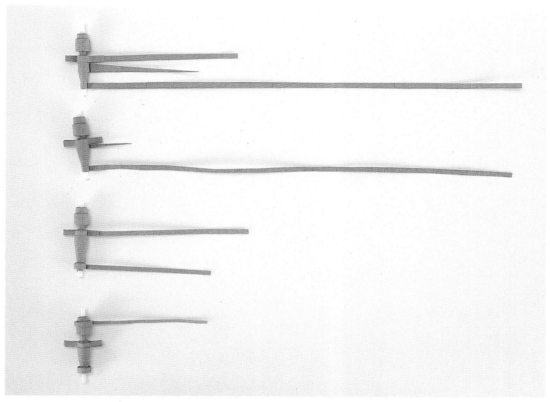

### Steps for a Man Bead Continued

4. Start gluing and pinching to form two arms.

5. After completing the arms, finish rolling the legs.

6. Roll a small disc for the feet.

7. To make a brim for the hat, roll a separate ⅛″ (.3cm) wide by 8″ (20.3cm) long strip around the head section, just below the hat crown.

### Steps for Painting a Man Bead

1. Assign a different color to each section of the figure.

2. Make stripes on the hat brim, arms and legs. A small oval serves for the mouth.

3. Add dots on the hat crown and legs, and make the eyes.

### Eye Detail

1. Make a dot.

2. Add a tail to make a comma shape.

3. Make short lines at the end of the comma.

4. Add a dot of highlight in the middle.

# A Woman Bead

For those of us who still like to play dress-up, this woman is irresistible. The most elaborate version pictured here boasts a three-tiered skirt made of three short, wide cone shapes. To puff up the sleeves, form the arms as usual and then roll a very small round bead around each. The scallops on her hat brim are made with the same method used to form the flower figure in chapter three, using very short petals.

The sample bead has a three-tiered hat just like the one worn by one of the head variations. To keep the hat in proportion to the rest of the figure, each of the tiers is a scant ⅛″ (.3cm). A narrow brim is also included in this unit; it can be made wider simply by adding another strip of paper.

**NOTE: Diagram is not proportional.**

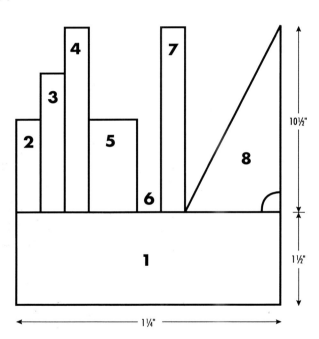

**Diagram for a Woman Bead**

1. *Base.* The base is 1¼″ (3.2cm) wide by 1½″ (3.8cm) long.
2. *Top Tier Hat.* The top tier of the hat is a scant ⅛″ (.3cm) wide by 2½″ (6.4cm) long.
3. *Middle Tier Hat.* The middle tier is a scant ⅛″ (.3cm) wide by 5½″ (14cm) long.
4. *Bottom Tier Hat.* The bottom tier is a scant ⅛″ (.3cm) wide by 10½″ (26.7cm) long.
5. *Head.* The head is ¼″ (.6cm) wide by 4½″ (11.4cm) long.
6. *Neck.* The neck is a ⅛″ (.3cm) empty space.
7. *Arms.* The arms are ⅛″ (.3cm) wide by 10½″ (26.7cm) long.
8. *Skirt.* The skirt is a right triangle, ½″ (1.3m) wide × 10½″ (26.7cm) long. Instead of cutting it to a point, blunt the tip to a width of ⅛″ (.3cm).
9. *Fringe.* The skirt fringe is a separate ⅛″ (.3cm) by 12″ (30.5m) strip.

### Steps for a Woman Bead

1. Roll the base onto the form.
2. Begin rolling the hat/head unit, stopping at each tier to glue down the "step."
3. Roll the skirt into a cone.
4. Glue and pinch two flat beads for the arms.
5. Roll a strip ⅛″ (.3cm) wide several times around the base of the skirt to form a fringe.

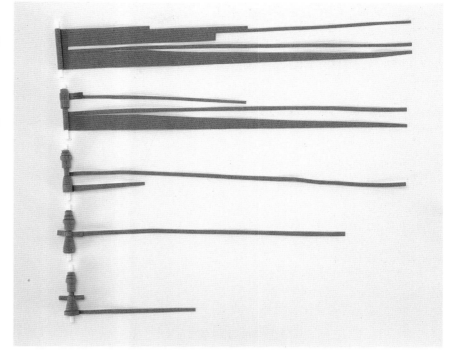

### Steps for Painting a Woman Bead

1. Assign a different color to each section.
2. Decorate the dress with zigzags and the fringe with stripes; add a dot for the mouth and two larger dots for the eyes.
3. Add more layers of stripes to the fringe; put buttons on the dress; decorate the hat with dots and stripes and complete the eyes.

### Eye Detail

1. Make a large dot.
2. Outline the dot.
3. Put a small dot inside.
4. Make small lines for eyelashes.

# The Gator Bead

This four-legged creature is the model for many others of similar ilk. Use your imagination and change the length or breadth of the head or body, add ears, a fin, or a nose, shorten the tail or cut it off all together, and create a whole new animal.

For the gator, a long right triangle makes a cone shaped head, the front feet are two flat beads, and the tapered body is formed from a trapezoid. The rear feet and tail are three flat beads.

NOTE: Diagram is not proportional.

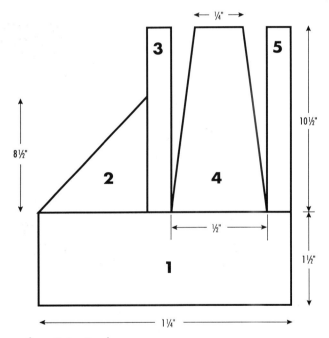

**Diagram for a Gator Bead**

1. *Base.* The base is 1¼″ (3.2cm) wide by 1½″ (3.8cm) long.
2. *Head.* The head is a right triangle ½″ (1.3cm) wide by 8½″ (21.6cm) long.
3. *Front Legs.* The front legs are ⅛″ (.3cm) wide by 10½″ (26.7cm) long. Additional ⅛″ (.3cm) wide strips may be added to make the legs and tail stronger.
4. *Body.* The body is a trapezoid, ½″ (1.3cm) wide at the bottom and ¼″ (.6cm) at the top by 10½″ (26.7cm) long.
5. *Rear Legs and Tail.* The rear legs and tail are ⅛″ (.3cm) wide by 10½″ (26.7cm) long.

# Steps for a Gator Bead

**1 Head**
Roll the head into a cone shape.

**2 Front Legs**
Roll the strip for the front legs four or five times around the base. Then begin to glue and pinch two flat beads about ¼″ (.6cm) long into shape. Position them well under the body, so the figure can stand by itself.

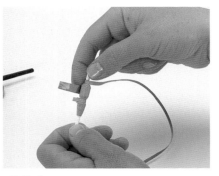

**3 Body**
Roll the body, allowing the trapezoid shape to spiral evenly on both sides.

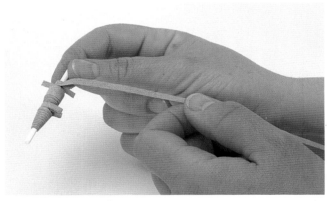

**4 Rear Legs and Tail**
Roll the last strip four or five times around the base. Then glue and pinch three flat beads—two for the rear legs and one perpendicular to the back for the tail.

## Steps for Painting a Gator Bead

1. Apply a base coat.
2. Make bold zigzags on the body and tail. Three short stripes serve for the feet. The nose is a long stripe with a dot at the end.
3. Add contrasting dots to the zigzags and make the mouth and eyes.

## Mouth Detail

1. Make a short zigzag in white to start the teeth.
2. Add a parallel zigzag below.
3. Fill in the zigzags.
4. Outline the zigzags in red.

# The Cat Bead

An honorary member of the gator family, the cat comes with a shorter cone for the head and a shorter, rounder body. This well-fed physique seems perfectly natural to me, since my model is a sixteen-year-old Rubenesque fellow who likes his chow. You can render him Stairmasteresque by using a short trapezoid for the body instead of the long triangle used here.

The ears also help distinguish the cat from the gator. They are two very short Flat Beads, made of a ⅛″ (.3cm) wide strip positioned between the head and front legs.

**Diagram for a Cat Bead**

1. *Base.* The base is ⅞″ (2.2cm) wide by 1½″ (3.8cm) long.

2. *Head.* The head is a right triangle, ¼″ (.6cm) wide by 8″ (20.3cm) long.

3. *Ears.* The ears are ⅛″ (.3cm) wide by 10½″ (26.7cm) long.

4. *Front Legs.* The front legs are ⅛″ (.3cm) wide by 10½″ (26.7cm) long.

5. *Body.* The body is an isosceles triangle, ¼″ (.6cm) wide by 9″ (22.9cm) long. The tip is slightly blunted to avoid making the body look too pointy in the middle.

6. *Rear Legs and Tail.* The rear legs and tail are ⅛″ (.3cm) wide by 10½″ (26.7cm) long.

NOTE: Diagrams are not proportional.

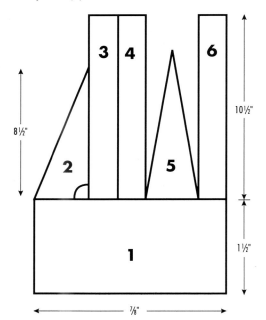

## Steps for a Cat Bead

1. Roll a cone shape for the head.
2. Roll the strip for the ears four or five times around the base, then begin to pinch them into shape as two ⅛" (.3cm) tall flat beads.
3. Keep the point of the isosceles triangle evenly in the middle while rolling the body.
4. Roll the last strip four or five times before making the rear legs and tail as three flat beads.

## Steps for Painting a Cat Bead

1. Make dots on the body and an oval for the eye.
2. Put dots in the dots, outline the eye and add a triangle for the nose.
3. Fill in the body with smaller dots and outline the nose. Add whiskers, eyelashes and a dot in the eye.

# The Pig Bead

With his round head and round body, the pig is little more than a bead with legs. A short, round nose is his defining characteristic, made of a small disc shape parked against his face. He has a much shorter tail than the cat and gator. As a more realistic alternative to the flat tail, a small piece of twisted tissue paper can be glued strategically on his rear.

This stubborn little fellow loses his piggishness when I paint him any color but pink. He seems much more comfortable with his normal skin and black trotters, though a belly full of stars and four striped socks don't seem to throw him off too much.

NOTE: Diagrams are not proportional.

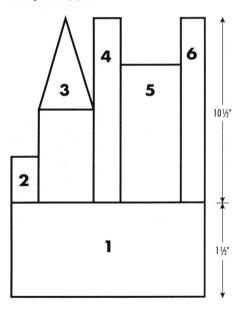

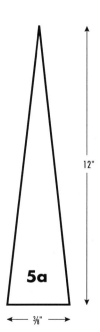

**Diagram for a Pig Bead**

1. *Base.* The base is 1″ (2.5cm) wide by 1½″ (3.8cm) long.
2. *Nose.* The nose is ⅛″ (.3cm) wide by 2½″ (6.4cm) long.
3. *Head.* The head is a ¼″ (.6cm) wide by 3″ (7.6cm) long isosceles triangle perched on a 7½″ (19.1cm) long extension.
4. *Front Legs.* The front legs are ⅛″ (.3cm) wide by 10½″ (26.7cm) long.
5. *Body Extension.* An extension ⅜″ (1.0cm) wide by 4″ (10.2cm) long.
5a. *Body.* The body is a ⅜″ (1.0cm) wide by 12″ (30.5cm) long isosceles triangle attached to a 4″ (10.2cm) long base.
6. *Rear Legs and Tail.* The rear legs and tail are ⅛″ (.3cm) wide by 10½″ (26.7cm) long.

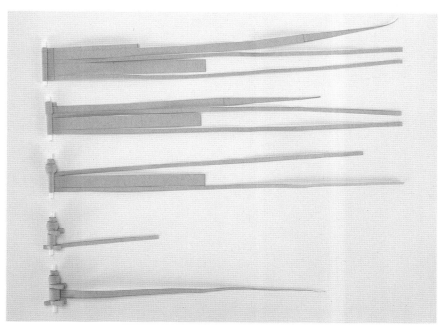

### Steps for a Pig Bead

1. Roll the base onto the stick.
2. Begin rolling the nose/head unit, stopping to glue down the nose. Continue rolling the head, keeping the tip of the triangle in the middle.
3. Glue and pinch the front legs into shape as two flat beads.
4. After rolling the extension for the body, form the rear legs and tail as three flat beads.
5. Add the 12″ (30.5cm) long triangle to fatten the body. As you roll it, keep the tip evenly centered.

### Steps for Painting a Pig Bead

1. Make a large dot for the eyes and an "X" to mark each foot.
2. Put another dot in the eye. Fill in the "X" marks on each foot. Stripe the legs and outline stars on the body.
3. Add a third dot to the eye and tiny lines for eyelashes. Fill in the stars. Make a dot for the nose, a curve for the mouth and a curlicue for the tail.

# The Flat Monster Bead

This creature came to me in a dream. His body is a ½″ (1.3cm) wide flat bead, which I used as a base for attaching arms and legs made of ⅛″ (.3cm) wide flat beads. A more involved version of this bead-on-bead construction technique is illustrated by the tapestry necklace pictured in the Gallery of Ideas.

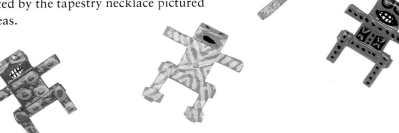

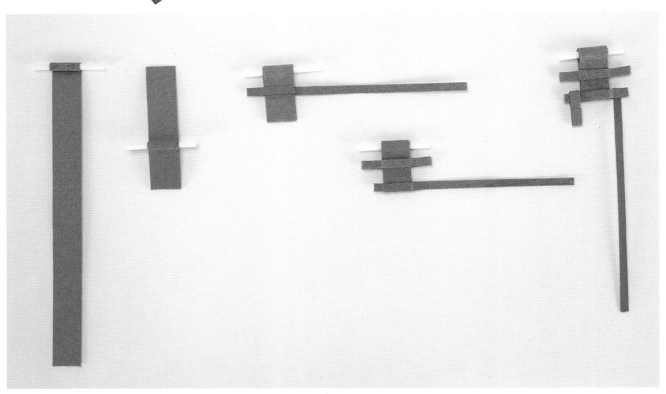

**Steps for a Monster Bead**

1. Roll a ½″ (1.3cm) wide by 12″ (30.5cm) long strip of paper four or five times around a stick to make a slim cylinder shape.

2. Glue and pinch the rest of the strip to make a flat bead. The total length of the bead, including the cylinder part, is about 1″ (2.5cm) in this sample. Continue to glue and pinch the strip, until the bead is about eight layers thick.

3. Attach a ⅛″ (.3cm) by 12″ (30.5cm) strip of paper to the flat part of the bead, about ¼″ (.6cm) below the cylinder part. Use this to make two flat beads for the arms. In this sample, the arms are about ⅜″ (.3cm) long.

4. Flush with the bottom of the bead, position another ⅛″ (.3cm) by 12″ (30.5cm) strip to make two short hips. They are about ⅛″ (.3cm) long, just enough to accommodate the legs.

5. Attach a ⅛″ (.3cm) by 10″ (25.4cm) strip to each hip and make two flat beads for the legs. Including the hip joint, the finished legs measure ⅝″ (1.6cm) long.

### Steps for Painting a Monster Bead

1. Highlight the sections of the body with small dots. Make two large dots for the eyes and an oval for the mouth.
2. Outline the mouth and eyes and add two squares on the chest.
3. Add another dot and eyelashes to the eyes; draw lines for the teeth; and decorate each square with an "X" dotted in the middle.

# The Snake Bead

The snake anticipates some of the techniques we explore in the next chapter. The snake shape is built by spiraling a ⅛″ (.3cm) strip of paper around a cylinder base and adding three more layers to the spiral to build three dimensions.

The head and tail are constructed like flat beads, but with one difference. Instead of rolling and folding a single strip of paper several times around the bead, the strip has to be cut off and restarted for each layer. Otherwise, the strip will crisscross instead of aligning into layers.

While the figure itself doesn't appear to allow much opportunity for variation, the snake will dramatically alter his appearance depending on the shape of the base upon which he sits, like the flat bead pictured here.

## Steps for a Snake Bead

**1 Cylinder Bead**
Make a cylinder bead from a 1¼″ (3.2cm) wide by 6″ (15.2cm) long strip of paper.

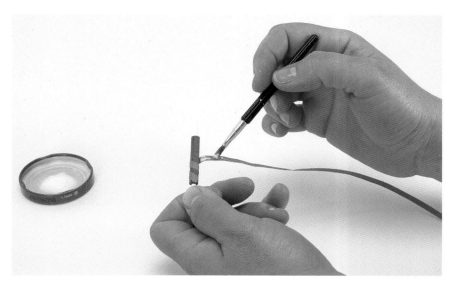

## 2 Spiral
Beginning at one end of the cylinder, spiral a ⅛″ (.3cm) by 12″ (30.5cm) strip of paper around it. Glue the strip thoroughly to prevent it from slipping.

## 3 Tail
When the spiral reaches the other end of the bead, don't trim off the excess. Glue and pinch it to start a flat bead about ¼″ (.6cm) long. This is the tail.

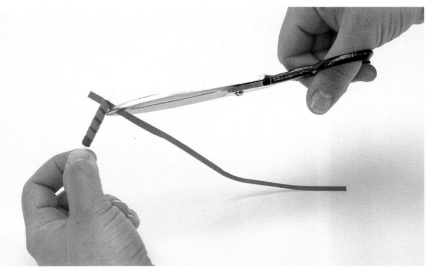

## 4 Trim
After pinching the strip back to meet the cylinder base, trim the excess off at a sharp angle. This leaves just a very short, angled bit of the strip to glue down to the cylinder base.

# Snake Bead

## 5 Layer and Spiral
Layer the remainder of the strip exactly over the first spiral, beginning at the back of the tail (the angled edges will just about match). Glue and pinch the strip over the tail, then continue spiraling back up the cylinder base.

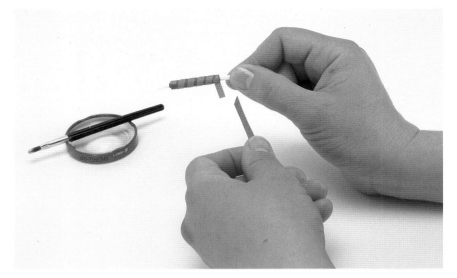

## 6 Neck
At the other end of the cylinder base, glue and pinch the strip to start a flat bead for the neck. This should measure about ⅜″ (1.0cm) long. Trim off the excess at an angle as in step four, and start layering on another strip as in step five. Repeat these steps until the body spiral has four layers of paper on it, making the neck and tail a sturdy eight layers thick.

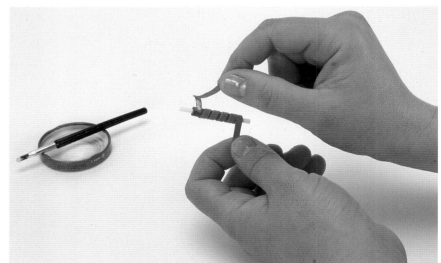

## 7 Head and Tongue
Once the body, neck and tail are formed, roll a small (¼″ [.6cm] wide by 6″ [15.2cm] long) isosceles triangle around the neck to make a head. About ⅛″ (.3cm) of the neck should project from the head, making the tongue.

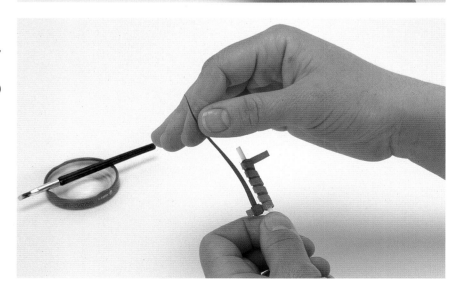

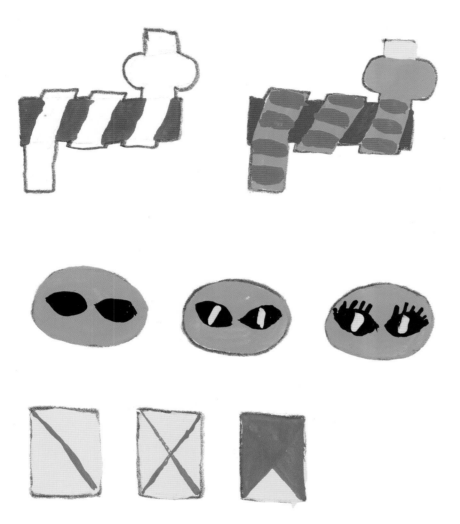

### Steps for Painting a Snake Bead

1. Paint the cylinder, continuing up the sides of the spiral.
2. Paint the head and body one color. Use a contrasting color for the tongue. Add stripes to the body.
3. Add more layers of stripes to the body and make the tongue and eyes.

### Eye Detail

1. Make two ovals.
2. Put a stripe in each oval.
3. Add eyelashes.

### Tongue Detail

1. Make a diagonal line across the tongue.
2. Make the opposite diagonal to form four triangles.
3. Fill in three of the triangles.

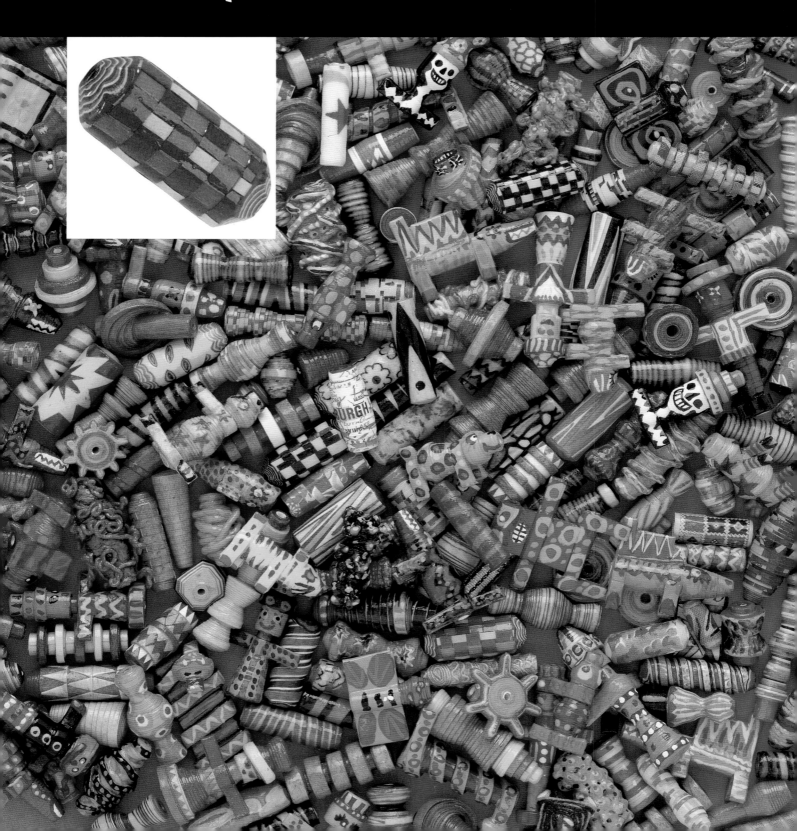

# CHAPTER FIVE

# The Sophisticated Bead

*I*n this chapter construction paper will again deliver on the promise of rare beauty hidden among its sheets. A slight alteration in the basic construction method—building shapes with short strips of paper instead of long ones—produces intricate silhouettes and elaborate color arrangements.

Because the color of the paper is so important, it's helpful to purchase two or even three packs of construction paper from different manufacturers, for a wider selection. An even greater variety is available at some art stores. Colored shopping bags from department stores and boutiques are other good sources. Gift wrap and other decorative paper are optional in this chapter, and can be used for accents.

A utility knife is highly recommended for some of the later projects in this chapter, but slight modifications in the procedure can allow for its absence.

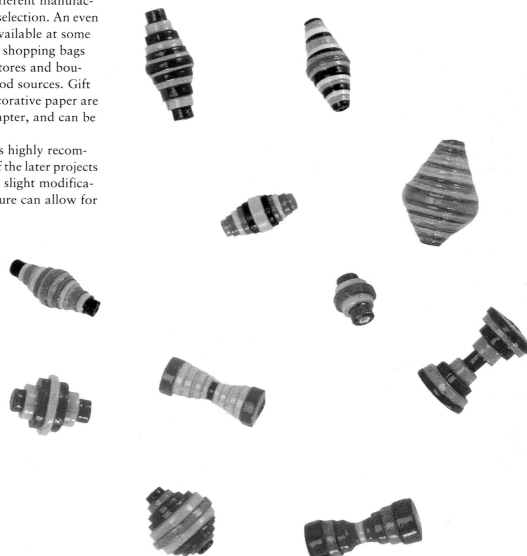

# Intricate Bead

This bead is shaped with a series of very short strips in contrasting colors, each slightly narrower than the preceding one. Each strip is just long enough to roll around the bead twice. In this sample, each color is ⅛″ (.3cm) narrower than the one below. A more delicate look can be achieved by graduating the strips in the smallest increments possible, 1/16″ (.2cm) or even less, and rolling each only one time around the bead.

## Steps for an Intricate Bead

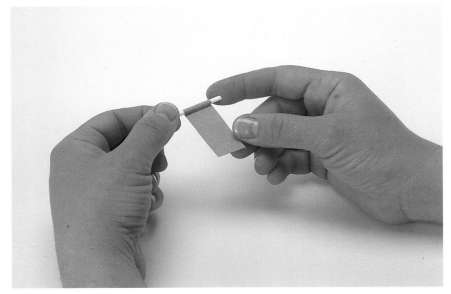

**1 Cylinder Bead**
Make a slim cylinder bead from a ¾″ (1.9cm) wide by 3″ (7.6cm) long rectangle.

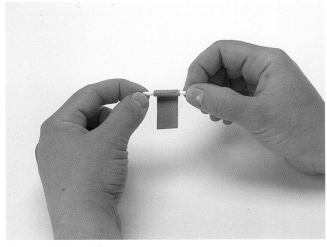

**2 Contrasting Color**
Attach a contrasting color, ⅝″ (1.6cm) wide by about 2″ (5.1cm) long, centering it evenly over the cylinder base. For ease of handling, this strip is longer than needed.

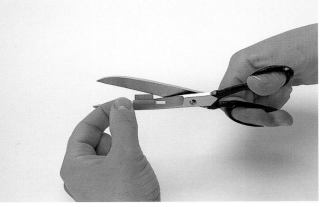

**3 Trim**
After rolling the strip twice around the cylinder base, trim off the excess. Each of the following colors will be exactly two layers around the bead.

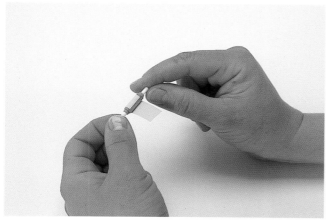

**4** **Third Color**
Add a third color, ½″ (1.3cm) wide by 2″ (5.1cm) long, centering it evenly over the preceding color. Trim off the excess.

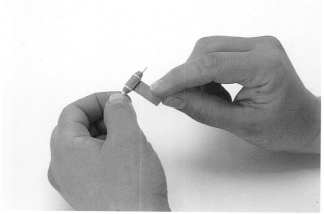

**5** **Fourth Color**
In the same manner, add a fourth color, ⅜″ (1.0cm) wide.

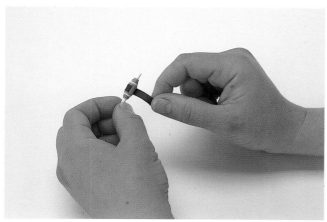

**6** **Fifth Color**
The fifth color is ¼″ (.6cm) wide . . .

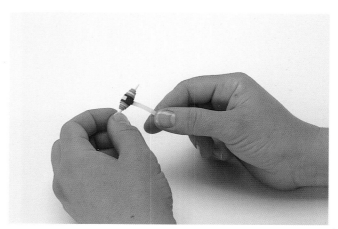

**7** **Finish**
. . . and the last is ⅛″ (.3cm) wide.

**Stages of Development** This is how the same bead looks in all its stages of development. Follow this shorthand format to make the other beads in this chapter.

# Intricate Corset Shape

Like the basic round bead, the Corset and other bead
shapes can be constructed with the short-strip method.
Centering the graduated series of strips approximates the
basic round bead shape; positioning it flush with one
side will produce a cone shape.

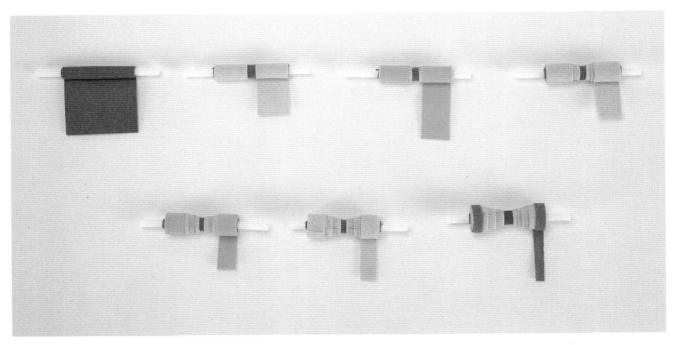

**Steps for an Intricate Corset Bead**

1. Make a cylinder base from a 1″ (2.5cm)
   wide by 2″ (5.1cm) long rectangle.

2. Add two ⁷⁄₁₆″ (1.1cm) wide by 2″
   (5.1cm) long strips. One side of each
   strip should be flush with each end of
   the cylinder, leaving an empty space on
   the base between them. Roll each strip
   twice around the base and trim off the
   excess.

3. In the same manner, add two ³⁄₈″
   (1.0cm) wide strips.

4. The third color is ⁵⁄₁₆″ (.8cm) wide . . .

5. . . . the fourth color is ¼″ (.6cm)
   wide . . .

6. . . . fifth is ³⁄₁₆″ (.5cm) wide . . .

7. . . . and the sixth is ⅛″ (.3cm) wide.

# Tiered Bead

For a more stripped-down, angular look layer strips on five or more times each, instead of only two.

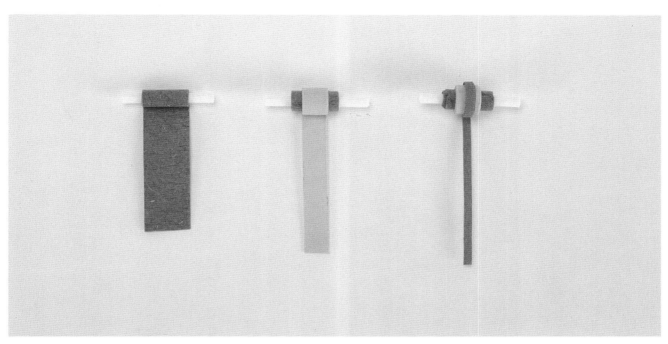

**Steps for a Tiered Bead**

1. The cylinder base is a ½″ (1.3cm) wide by 4″ (10.2cm) long strip.

2. The next color is a ¼″ (.6cm) wide by 6″ (15.2cm) long strip. Roll it around the base, centering it evenly in the middle and using the entire strip.

3. In the same manner, add a ⅛″ (.3cm) wide by 8″ (20.3cm) long strip.

# Firecracker Bead

Wilder than their sedate cousins, these beads still adhere to the same principles of construction as the intricate bead. The accents come from trimming a zigzag into the edges of some of the strips.

Standard pinking shears and children's novelty scissors can make quick zigzags for an oversized bead. The beads pictured here, though, demand a tighter pattern, cut by hand with a pair of ordinary flat blade scissors.

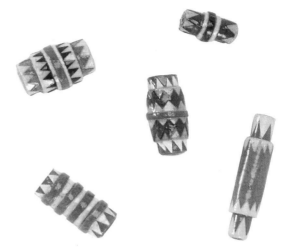

**Zigzags.** To cut a zigzag edge efficiently, first draw a line down the strip to mark the depth of the cuts (⅛″ [.3cm] in this sample). Then cut a series of *zigs* all the way down the edge of the strip. Turn the strip over and cut down the edge again to complete the *zags*.

### Steps for a Firecracker Bead

1. Make a cylinder base from a ¾″ (1.9cm) wide by 6″ (15.2cm) long rectangle.
2. Add one layer of contrasting color, ¾″ (1.9cm) wide, with the edges zigzagged to a depth of ⅛″ (.3cm) on each side.
3. Add another contrasting color, ½″ (1.3cm) wide by 3″ (7.6cm) long.
4. Add one layer, ½″ (1.3cm) wide, with the edges zigzagged ⅛″ (.3cm) deep.
5. Add one final zigzag layer, ¼″ (.6cm) wide.
6. Finish with one layer of a narrow strip, a scant ⅛″ (.3cm) wide.

# Firecracker Woman Bead

Use firecracker accents with the short-strip method to produce livelier forms. The beads pictured here mix elements of long triangles and short rectangles to plow a fertile field of design options.

*For the sake of clarity, the completed skirt has been left out of the second series of steps.*

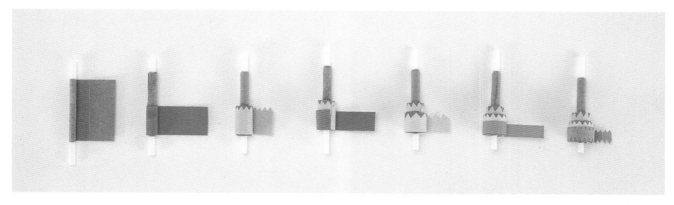

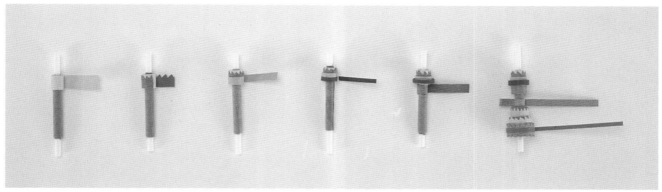

**Steps for a Firecracker Woman**

1. Make a cylinder base from a 1¼″ (3.2cm) wide by 2″ (5.1cm) long strip.
2. Start the skirt with a ⅝″ (1.6cm) wide by 8″ (20.3cm) long strip, positioned flush with one end of the bead.
3. Add one layer of ⅝″ (1.6cm) wide zig-zag trim . . .
4. . . . a ⅜″ (1.0cm) wide by 4″ (10.2cm) long strip . . .
5. . . . one layer of ⅜″ (1.0cm) wide trim . . .
6. . . . a ¼″ (.6cm) wide by 4″ (10.2cm) long strip . . .
7. . . . and one layer of ¼″ (.6cm) wide trim, with both edges of the strip cut in a zigzag.
8. On the opposite end of the base, start the hat with a ¼″ (.6cm) wide by 3″ (7.6cm) long strip. Position the strip flush with the end of the bead.
9. Add one ¼″ (.6cm) wide layer of zig-zag trim . . .
10. . . . two layers of a ⅛″ (.3cm) wide strip . . .
11. . . . and two layers of a scant ⅛″ (.3cm) wide strip.
12. Make the head from a ¼″ (.6cm) wide by 5″ (12.7cm) long strip positioned flush against the hat brim.
13. Pinch two flat beads for the arms, from a ⅛″ (.3cm) by 12″ (30.5cm) strip. Add a very narrow strip to highlight the middle of the skirt.

# Spiral Bead

In this group of beads, the short-strip method is modified to allow glimpses of the cylinder base below. A graduated series of narrow strips are layered in a spiral around a cylinder base. The snake figure described in chapter four is constructed along similar lines. The top layer is a good place to embellish with a strip of decorative paper.

A utility knife comes in handy here because it trims the ends of the bead through all the layers of the base and spiral in one quick maneuver. A neatly finished bead can still be accomplished without a knife, albeit at a slower pace, by trimming each layer off with scissors before gluing down the next layer.

## Steps for a Spiral Bead

### 1 Cylinder Base
Make a cylinder base. In this sample, the base is constructed of three 1″ (2.5cm) wide strips. The bottom strip is 3″ (7.6cm) long, the middle is 2″ (5.1cm), and the topmost is 3″ (7.6cm). If a utility knife is not to be used, a plain monocolor base, 1″ (2.5cm) wide by 8″ (20.3cm) long, will suffice.

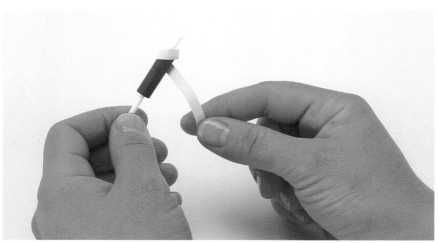

### 2 Spiral
Spiral a ³⁄₁₆″ (.5cm) wide by about 6″ (15.2cm) long strip of contrasting paper around the base. If you have a utility knife, let the beginning and end of the strip hang off the end of the base. It will be trimmed when the bead is complete. Otherwise, trim the ends with a scissors now.

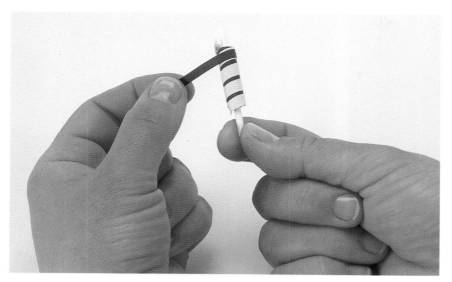

**3 Second Spiral**
Layer on a second, slightly narrower spiral.

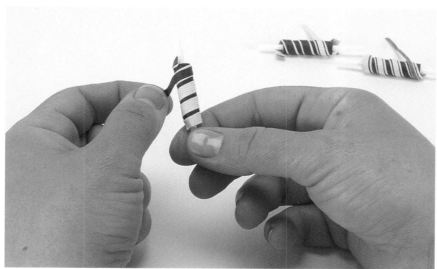

**4 More Spirals**
Add more spiral layers, each a little narrower than the one below.

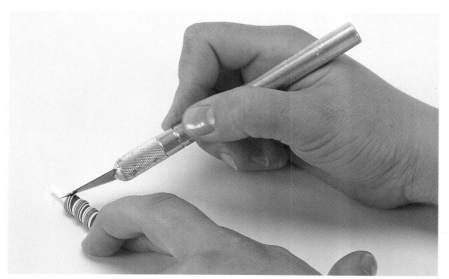

**5 Trim Ends**
With a utility knife, trim through all layers of the spiral at each end of the bead. Trim down through the cylinder base to reveal the different layers of color used there.

# Triangle Variation

The unusual design of this bead springs from the same principle used in the spiral bead—one simple shape layered at intervals on a cylinder base. This bead uses a series of triangles.

The triangles are all the same size, but each layer is shifted slightly to allow the one beneath to show.

A utility knife again is a useful but ultimately nonessential tool. The ends of the bead can be neatened by trimming each layer with a scissors. Alternatively, tidy the ends by constructing other bead elements on top; the pink and purple bead shown here employs two cone shapes.

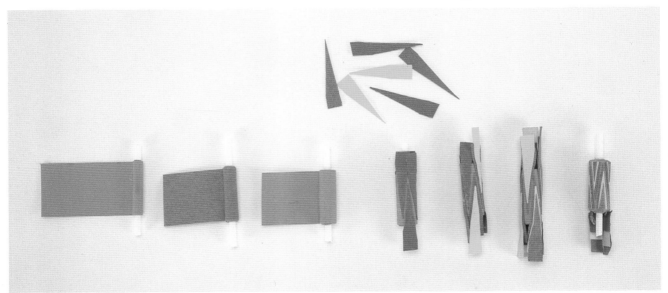

**Steps for a Triangle Variation**

1. Make a cylinder base. In this sample, the base is 1″ (2.5cm) wide.
2. Same as 1 above using a second color.
3. Same as 1 above using a third color.
4. Cut a number of small isosceles triangles, about ¼″ (.6cm) wide at the base by about 1¼″ (3.2cm) long. To save time, cut them by eye; the measurements need not be precise. This bead requires eight triangles in each of the three colors.

5. Apply the first layer of triangles lengthwise along the cylinder base. There should be room for four at each end. When gluing on a triangle, hold it at the base and position it so the tip rests about ⅛″ (.3cm) away from the other end of the bead. Let the excess base drape over the end. If you have a utility knife, trim the excess after the bead is completed; otherwise, trim it flush with scissors now.

6. Position the other four triangles with their bases at the other end, so their tips fill the empty space between the first set, with a slim border of the cylinder base showing between.
7. Add a second layer of triangles in a contrasting color. Shift them slightly toward the ends of the beads, allowing a narrow border of the first layer of triangles to show. In the same manner, apply a third layer of triangles.
8. Trim the ends with a utility knife.

# Striped Variation

The elegance of stripes is such that a single layer is sufficient to produce a satisfying design in short order. However, as with so many other beads, the visual rewards of
patience are ample. I recommend a minimum of three
layers.

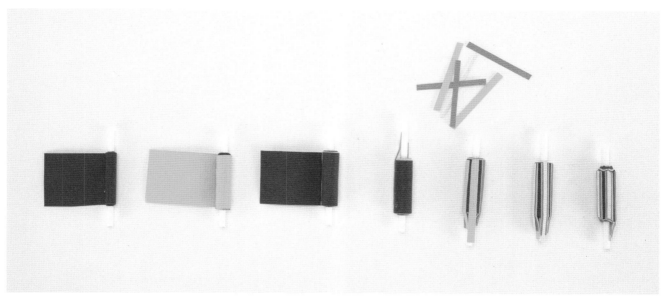

**Steps for Striped Variation**

1. Make a cylinder base that is 1″ (2.5cm) wide and 4″ (10.2cm) long.

2. Add a second cylinder base of a contrasting color that is 1″ (2.5cm) wide and 2″ (5.1cm) long.

3. Add a third color cylinder base that is 1″ (2.5cm) wide and 2″ (5.1cm) long.

4. Begin to glue ⅛″ (.3cm) wide strips of contrasting paper lengthwise along the cylinder base. Place them close together, allowing just a small band of the base color to show between.

5. Add another layer that is slightly narrower than the one below.

6. Same as 5 above.

7. Trim through all the layers with a utility knife.

# Woven Bead

The top layer of this bead is woven from paper strips using the same over-under method that a summer camp counselor demonstrates for making place mats. The only difference is the width of the strips. A width of ⅛″ (.3cm) is fine for practice; the closer to 1/16″ (.2cm), the more startling the results.

A monocolor base is adequate to support a fine looking woven bead. The sample bead illustrated here sports an over-the-top base composed of about fifteen layers, with two colors alternating on each layer. There's a long way and a short way to accomplish this. The long way—very long—is to apply each layer individually. The short way is to roll two contrasting strips around the bead at the same time. Roll and glue the strips bit by bit—about ½″ (1.3cm) at a time—to prevent the two layers from wrinkling and buckling.

At first, the tediousness of this effort may not seem to justify the results, but bear with it. The first time I rolled two strips at once, it seemed so hopeless that I didn't make another attempt for more than a year. Now I routinely use this method. With practice, the pace quickens and the spectacular climax is well worth the extra work. Once fluent in two colors, try adding a third, fourth or even more. The alternating colors make a peerless base for any bead, especially for the carved work described in chapter six.

## Steps for a Woven Bead

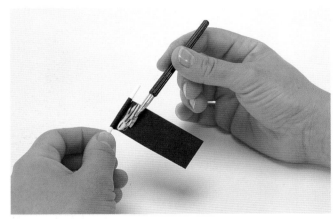

**1 Cylinder Base**
Using a 1″ (2.5cm) wide by 12″ (30.5cm) long strip of paper, start a cylinder base. Roll the strip once or twice around the base. Apply glue over the next ½″ (1.3cm) or so, but don't roll it yet.

**2 Contrast**
Place a contrasting 1″ (2.5cm) wide by 12″ (30.5cm) long strip over the glued section.

## 3 Glue

Glue ½″ (1.3cm) or so of this second strip, but do not roll it yet.

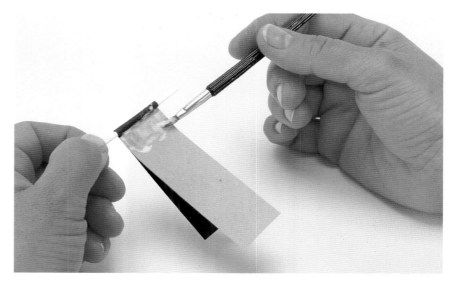

## 4 Bend and Glue Strips

Bend the second strip (the pink one here) out of the way, letting it begin to roll around the cylinder base, and glue another ½″ (1.3cm) or so of the first strip. Then press the first strip (the black one) up to follow the second strip around the cylinder base. Continue in this manner, gluing both strips a bit at a time (bending the second strip away to reach the first), until about 2″ (5.1cm) remain to be rolled.

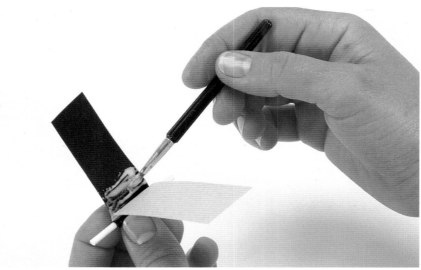

## 5 Trim One Strip

Trim off the excess from one of the strips. In this sample, the second strip is trimmed to leave the black.

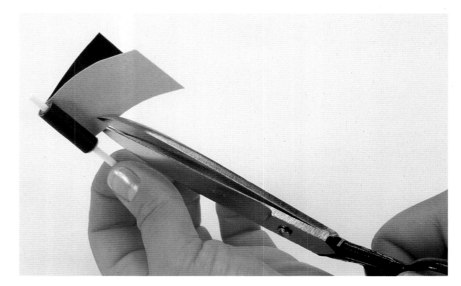

# Woven Bead

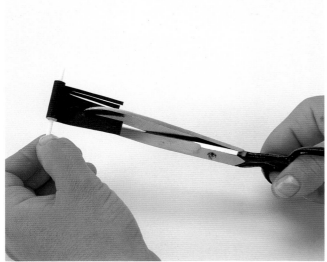

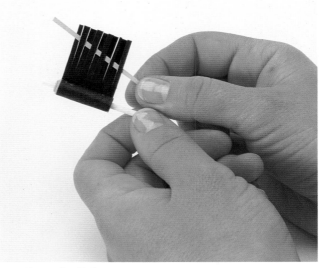

**6 Cut Warp**
Make lengthwise cuts in the remaining strip. This forms the warp of the woven section. There should be enough room to make at least seven or eight cuts; to save time, cut them by eye. This section should be about 1½" (3.8cm) long, or long enough to go around the bead once.

**7 Weave the Weft**
Start weaving narrow strips of a contrasting color, about ¹⁄₁₆" (.2cm) wide by 2" (5.1cm) long, through the warp. These strips are the "weft."

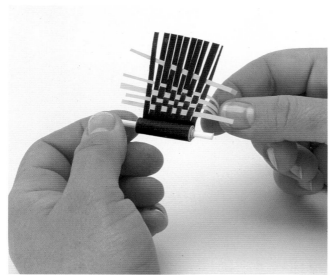

**8 Push and Weave**
After weaving each strip, gently push it down toward the cylinder base section. Push the strips as close together as possible. Keep weaving strips until there are enough to form a complete layer around the cylinder.

**9 Glue and Trim Weft**
Secure the weft strips to the outermost warp strips with a small dot of glue at each end. If you don't have a utility knife, trim off the excess weft with a scissors now. Otherwise, wait until the bead is complete. The excess weft will be trimmed off when the ends are carved.

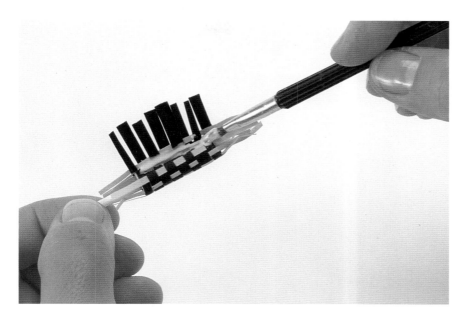

## 10 Glue
Glue the woven section around the cylinder base.

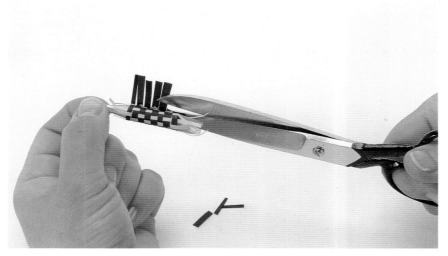

## 11 Trim Warp
Trim off the excess warp. A precisely matched checkerboard pattern is unlikely at this juncture, but such an imperfection is too slight to diminish the overall effect.

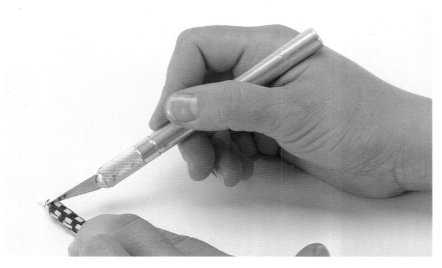

## 12 Taper Ends
Use a utility knife to taper the ends of the bead.

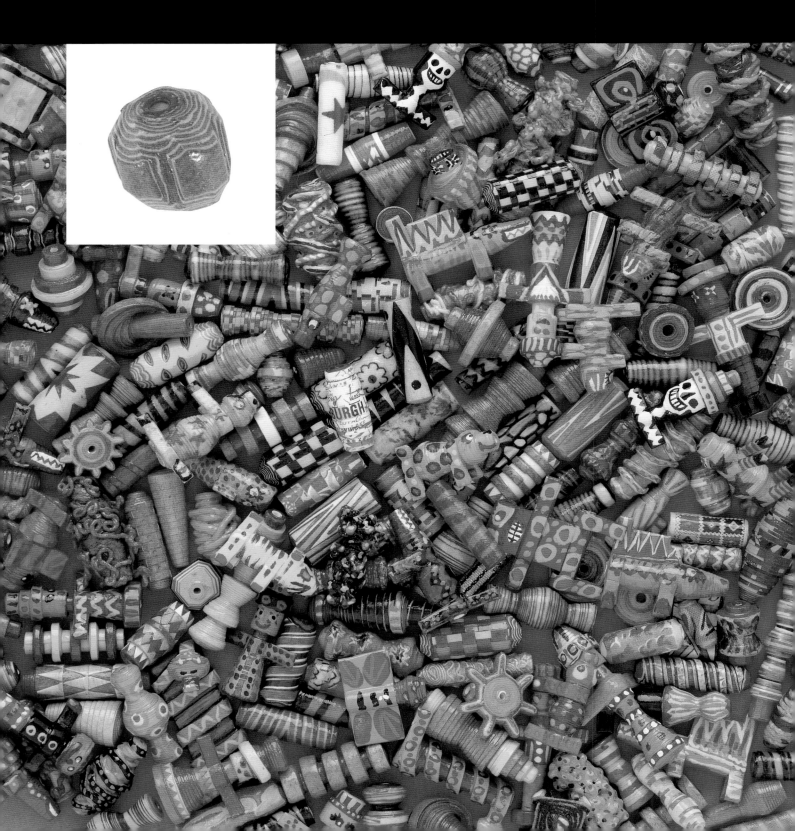

# CHAPTER SIX

# The Touchable Bead

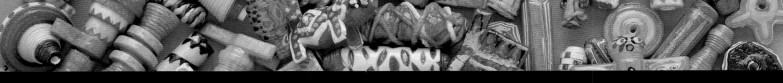

**E**verything has a texture, a surface that you feel when you touch it. The issue for bead design is just how much attention to draw to texture. In the preceding chapters, our beads have announced themselves with a symphony of meticulous wrapping and decorating that has overwhelmed the feel of the bead. Once coaxed out from the sheltering arms of form and color, texture becomes a compelling design element in its own right.

For the first group of beads in this chapter, the ever dependable construction paper will get yet another new treatment. A utility knife is indispensable for these projects. Also have a cutting board or a piece of cardboard on hand.

Colored shopping bags or any heavy paper can substitute for construction paper. Decorative papers are optional; they can be used as accents and highlights.

The later projects in the chapter call for white tissue paper and a set of paints, or a variety of colored tissue papers. Packs of colored tissue paper are available at craft shops. Any other thin, soft paper like colored napkins can substitute. If they have several layers, separate them. A utility knife isn't needed for the tissue paper projects.

# Notched Beads

The familiar cylinder base is now the jumping off point for carving instead of rolling. A paper cylinder is a comfortable object to whittle. A sharp utility knife cuts through it like butter, with a faint, enjoyable rasping sound. When made of layers of contrasting paper, a cylinder presents a twofold measure of pleasure—first, when the carving reveals the multicolored layers, and again when a coat of varnish makes the dull construction paper sparkle into life.

The cylinder base should be constructed to make the interior as solid as a piece of wood. Glue all of the strips of paper thoroughly—across their entire surface. Unglued sections may pop off like loose pieces of bark when the carving is under way.

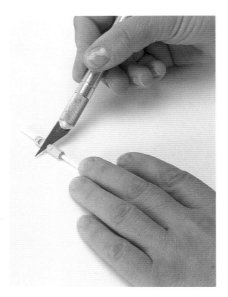

## Steps for a Notched Bead

### 1 Cylinder Base

Make a cylinder base of two or more colors. The top color should be just one layer. The base here is made of four 1″ (2.5cm) wide strips. The first three are 2″ (5.1cm) long. The final strip is just long enough to go around the bead once. Allow the glue to dry for about an hour before carving, giving it time to set. Don't let it sit overnight or the glue will become rock hard, making it difficult to carve.

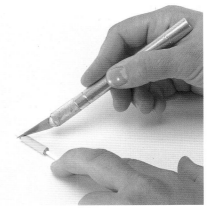

### 2 Trim

Trim the ends of the cylinder base.

### 3 Start Notch

Start a notch by cutting crosswise into the cylinder at a slight angle. Use a single firm, downward motion to make the cut. It should be deep enough to expose the most colors without weakening the structure of the bead.

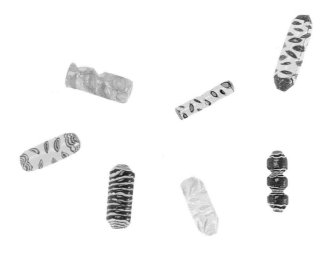

### 4 Complete Notch

Position the knife parallel to the first cut, about ⅛″ (.3cm) away, and complete the notch by making a second cut. Angle the knife so the two cuts meet at the bottom. A small wedge of paper should fall loose; if it stays attached, pry it out with the tip of the knife. Repeat steps three and four to make notches randomly across the entire surface of the bead. Alternatively, create specific patterns by arranging the notches in an orderly fashion.

# Grooved Bead

For a beginning whittler, lengthwise grooves are a bit trickier to manage than crosswise notches. The general method is the same, however. Each groove is made by two adjacent cuts running parallel to each other on the surface of the bead, but angled to meet several layers down.

## Steps for a Grooved Bead

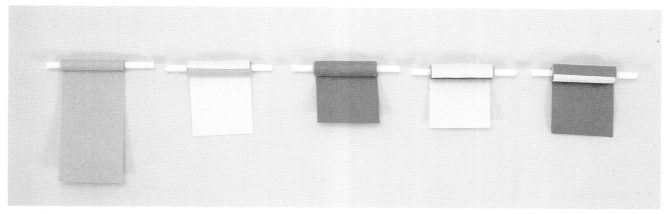

**1 Cylinder Base**
Make a cylinder base using two or more colors. This sample starts with a 1″ (2.5cm) by 5″ (12.7cm) base, then adds four single layers in alternating colors. Allow glue to set before carving.

**2 Start Groove**
Start a groove by making one deep, slightly angled cut down the entire length of the bead. This maneuver is easiest if you apply pressure to the tip of the blade rather than force the entire length of the blade down at once.

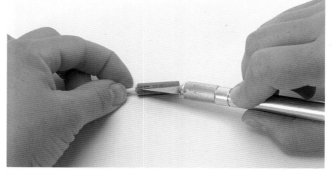

**3 Finish Groove**
Complete the groove by placing the knife parallel to the first cut and making a second cut, slightly angled so they meet below the surface. A long wedge of paper should fall out; if it doesn't, pry it out with the tip of the blade. Make lengthwise grooves all around the bead then trim the ends.

# Shaved Bead

In contrast to the precision required by the notched and grooved beads, shaved beads revel in a show of ragged patches of color. The pattern is transformed by the basic flat-across-the-surface whittling move. For ease of handling, though, it helps to hold the bead against a cutting board.

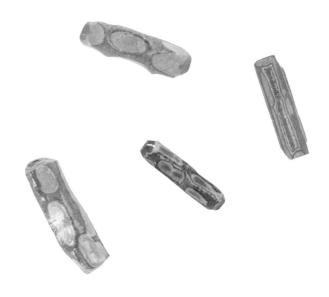

## Steps for a Shaved Bead

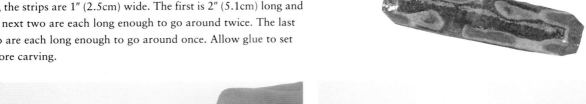

### 1 Cylinder Base

Make the cylinder base from at least three colors. In this sample, the strips are 1″ (2.5cm) wide. The first is 2″ (5.1cm) long and the next two are each long enough to go around twice. The last two are each long enough to go around once. Allow glue to set before carving.

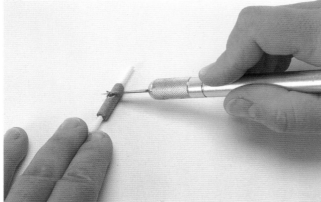

### 2 Shave

To start shaving, position the knife crosswise in the middle of the cylinder and lay the blade nearly flat against the surface. Shave down toward the end with one smooth, firm motion.

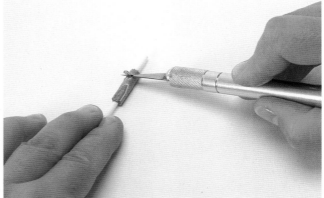

### 3 Turn Bead and Shave

Turn the bead around and start with the blade in the middle again, shaving toward the opposite end.

# Slit-and-Peel Bead

Of all the carved beads, this one calls for the greatest measure of care and precision. It's also the most unforgiving if there is inadequately glued paper in the cylinder base. If pieces do pop loose, the bead may be rescued by picking up the errant scrap on the point of a pin and gluing it back in place.

The only contrast that really matters in this bead is between the top layer of the cylinder base and the one below it. For this reason, the sample bead is made with a base of only two colors.

A third contrasting color at each end of the bead highlights the work in the middle. The bead on the far right in the array shown here uses a trapezoid base to accomplish this. Another method of framing the work is to start the cylinder base in a third color, then taper the ends of the completed bead with a utility knife to show it off.

## Steps for a Slit-and-Peel Bead

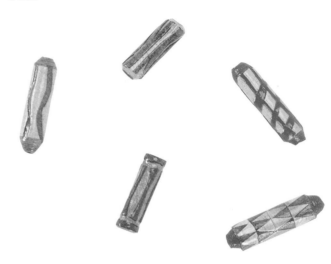

**1 Cylinder Base**
Make a cylinder base from 1″ (2.5cm) wide strips. The first strip is 6″ (15.2cm) long. The top strip is just long enough to go around once. Allow the glue to set before carving.

◄ **2 Slit Top Layer**
Using the tip of the blade, make a slit in the top layer from end to end, deep enough to penetrate the top layer completely and go partly into the next layer.

**3 Second Slit ►**
Make a second slit parallel to the first one. In this sample, the two slits are a scant ⅛″ (.3cm) apart.

**4 Reveal Contrasting Layer**
Use the tip of the blade to pry loose the top layer of paper between the two slits, revealing the contrasting layer beneath.

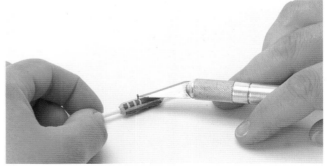

**5 Finish**
Continue to make sets of two slits on the bead, peeling out the narrow strip of paper between them.

# Complex Carving

Combining notches, grooves, shaves or the slit-and-peel method opens up a wealth of design possibilities. The sample bead here starts with a base of alternating colors using the technique described for the Woven Bead in chapter five. Then deep notches are cut, end to end in two continuous rows, to divide the bead surface into three sections. The middle section is slit laterally, at a slightly spiraled angle, to complete the design.

## Steps for a Carved Bead

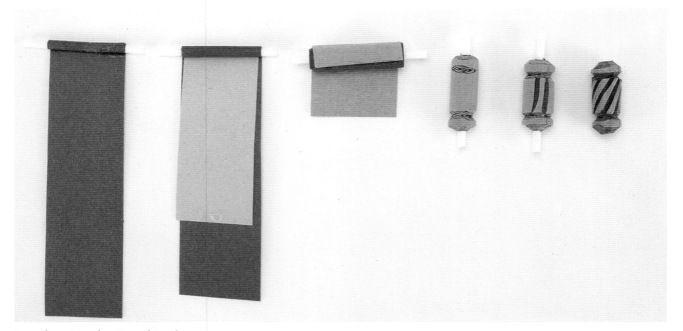

**Steps for a Complex Carved Bead**

1. To make the cylinder base featured here, start with a 1" (2.5cm) wide by 12" (30.5cm) long strip. Roll it only once or twice around the stick.

2. Attach a second 1" (2.5cm) wide by 12" (30.5cm) long strip in a contrasting color and roll the two strips together (for detailed instructions see the Woven Bead, chapter five).

3. After completing the two-color base, add a final, single layer in a third color.

4. Trim the ends of the bead to taper them slightly. About ⅛" (.3cm) from each end, make a crosswise series of deep notches overlapping each other.

5. Make parallel slits in the middle section of the bead and peel out the paper between.

6. Continue making parallel slits and peeling until the midsection is thoroughly striped.

# Stacked Bead

The stacked bead—true to its name—is the only bead in this book that involves no rolling. Small scraps of paper stacked atop one another is the mode of construction. Depending on the thickness of the paper, at least two layers of each color are needed to make a stripe that is wide enough to catch the eye.

After completing my first stacked bead, I vowed never again to subject myself to what seemed like the most laborious procedure, short of labor, of my life. But the siren call of its delicate stripes lured me irresistibly back for another try. By organizing the materials more efficiently, and cutting the paper by eye instead of measuring it, I refined the process to a pace that made the investment in time well worth the return.

A utility knife is needed to tidy the edges of the completed bead and show off the colored paper to its best advantage.

## Steps for a Stacked Bead

**1 Cut Scraps**
Cut a dozen or more small scraps of paper, about ½″ (1.3cm) square. For this sample, sixteen scraps are used. Cut them by eye to save time; they don't need to be measured exactly. The completed stack will be carved all around the edges.

**2 Arrange Scraps**
Organize the scraps according to their arrangement on the bead. This saves time searching for the right color and ensures that there are enough scraps to complete the design.

# Stacked Bead

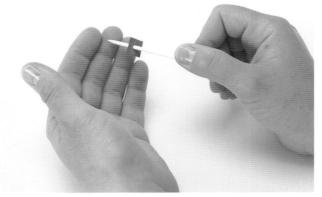

### 3 Soften Paper
Put a drop of water in the middle of each scrap. This softens the paper and makes the stacking process go more quickly.

### 4 Begin Stacking
Poke a stick through the middle of the first scrap. Trim a plastic swab or any stick with blunt ends to a sharp point for this maneuver.

### 5 Continue Stacking
Continue stacking scraps onto the stick, according to the sequence you laid out. Stack as many as will fit loosely on the stick. If there are leftovers, as here, they'll be put on later.

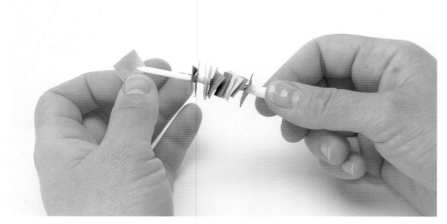

### 6 Glue
Dot one side of each scrap with glue.

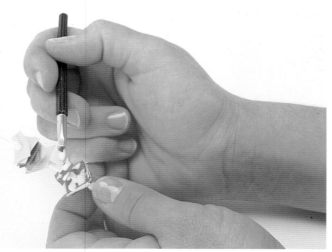

## 7 Squeeze

Squeeze all of the scraps tightly together between your fingers. Wipe off the glue that leaks from the sides.

## 8 Stack More

Stack the remaining scraps, glue and squeeze them together with the first group of scraps. Repeat as needed until all of the scraps are stacked on the stick.

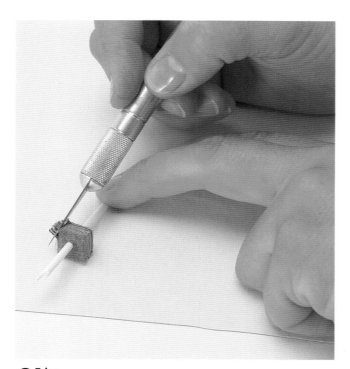

## 9 Trim

Wait about an hour for the glue to set and then trim the bead with a utility knife to tidy the edges.

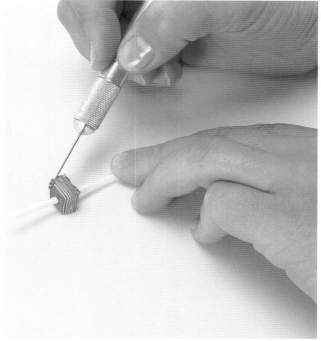

## 10 Trim Corners

To really show off the colors from all sides, round off the square by trimming its corners, continuing at an angle onto the top and bottom surfaces.

# Painted Tissue Spirals

Plain tissue paper, when cut into long strips, wrapped and twisted around a stick and painted, rivals plastic, glass or ceramic beads for color and style. The uneven texture and misshapen contour of tissue beads contributes an intriguing new look even to a simple painted design.

Firmness is important in a well-constructed tissue bead. The soft, pliable paper must be disciplined with a strong hand. A properly wrapped, generously glued tissue bead will dry as hard as a rock. Any lapse in resolve will reflect in a sponge-like feel to the finished bead.

The sample illustrated here uses green tissue purely for the sake of clarity. Plain white or any color will suffice. A set of paints is needed to decorate the bead.

## Steps for a Painted Tissue Spiral Bead

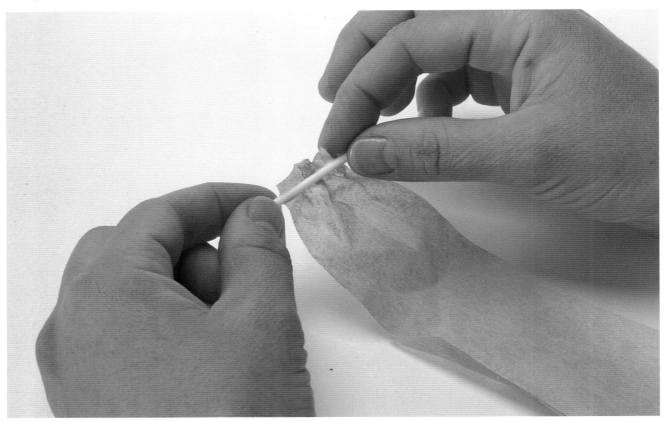

**1 Base**

Start the base of the bead with a long strip of plain tissue paper. In this sample, the strip is about 1½″ (3.8cm) wide by 18″ (45.7cm) long. Since tissue is too soft to measure and mark efficiently, cut the strip by eye.

Apply a generous amount of glue to the first ½″ (1.3cm) of one end of the strip. After positioning it on the stick, push it together slightly to approximate the length of the completed bead.

## 2 Wind, Twist and Glue

Begin winding the strip around the stick. Pull it firmly, twist it lightly and glue it generously to make the base sturdy and solid. If the tissue is wrapped lightly and glued inadequately, the completed bead will be soft and spongy.

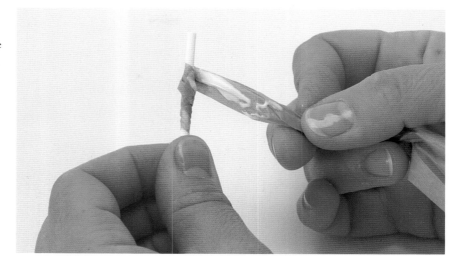

## 3 Build Shapes

Continue twisting and wrapping the tissue. By concentrating the tissue in one area or another, you can build different shapes. This sample has an hourglass form, achieved with a few extra twists and rolls at each end of the bead.

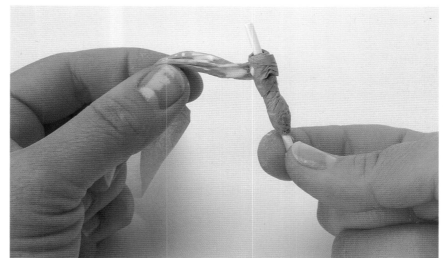

## 4 Prepare Tissue String

Twist another 1½" (3.8cm) wide strip of tissue into a long string. Wet your fingertips to make the string hold its shape. Don't use glue. The string unwinds a bit at this stage, but it will be tightened up as it is glued on the base.

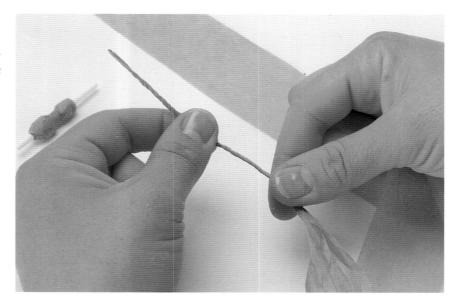

# Painted Tissue Spiral Bead

**5** **Glue Tissue String**
Glue one tip of the tissue string to one end of the bead. Hold it in place for a few minutes until the glue sets.

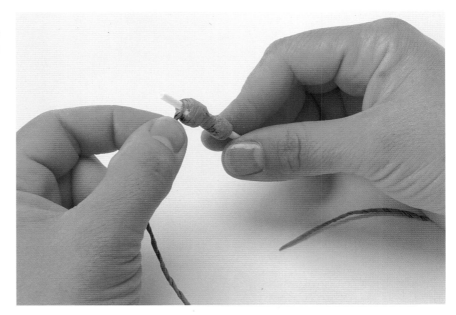

**6** **Spiral Tissue String**
Firmly spiral the string around the base, adding a few dots of glue as needed. Use glue sparingly, as excess on the surface can prevent paint from being absorbed evenly into the paper. To that end, dot the glue on the base and press the string over it. When the string reaches the other end of the base, trim the excess string and glue down the tip.

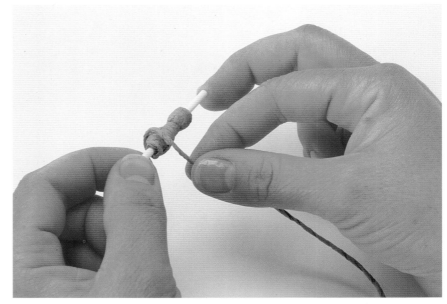

**Steps for Painting a Tissue Spiral Bead**
1. Let the completed bead dry.
2. Cover the bead with a base coat, working the pigment into all of the crevices.
3. Use a small brush to paint a continuous line on the top of the spiral.
4. Add dots to the spiral in another contrasting color.

# Colored Tissue Spirals

Colored tissue opens new boulevards in bead design. Free of paint, the texture of the tissue bursts forth in all its wrinkled glory. Thin strings of tissue in contrasting colors can be twisted together to form intricate spirals that would be difficult and time consuming to mimic with paint.

This sample bead demonstrates how tissue can perform not only in an asymmetrical, free-form style, but in a sleek, well tuned mode as well.

## Steps for a Colored Tissue Spiral Bead

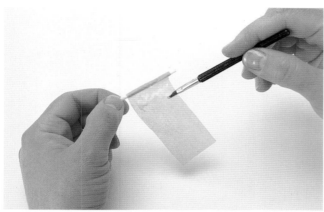

**1 Roll Base**
For this slim, elegant cylinder base start with a 2″ (5.1cm) wide by 6″ (15.2cm) long strip of tissue paper. It can be cut by eye. Roll it around the stick without twisting or pushing it together. Glue liberally.

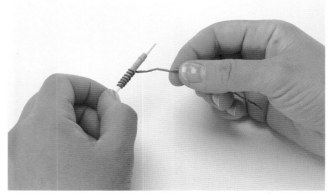

**2 Refine Base**
Push the completed base together between your fingertips. This shortens the bead, makes it slightly thicker and stronger and forms a subtle texture of fine wrinkles. Keep pushing until the base is the size you want for the finished bead. Wait a few minutes for the glue to dry. If it's too wet, the dye in the tissue paper might run when the contrasting color is spiraled on.

**3 Wrap and Spiral a Twisted String of Tissue**
Wrap a very thin, tightly twisted string of tissue in a contrasting color once around one end of the base. Then begin to spiral it toward the other end. Dot the base sparingly with glue to keep the spiral in place.

**4 Continue Spiral**
Continue spiraling the string. When it reaches the other end of the base, wrap it around once, trim off the excess and glue down the tip.

# Tissue Curlicues

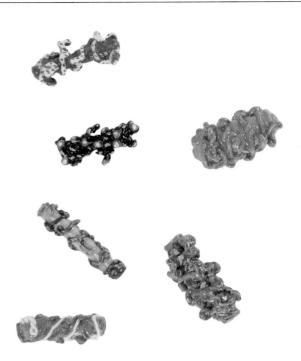

Twist a tissue string between your fingers a few extra times and it curls into a neat little loop. A series of loops entertains the eye with its convoluted antics. A coat of paint fills in the holes to produce an unusually deep, complex surface for further embellishment.

As with the tissue spirals, the most efficient way to glue down a curlicue is to put a small dot of glue on the base, then press the twisted tissue onto it.

## Steps for a Colored Tissue Curlicue Bead

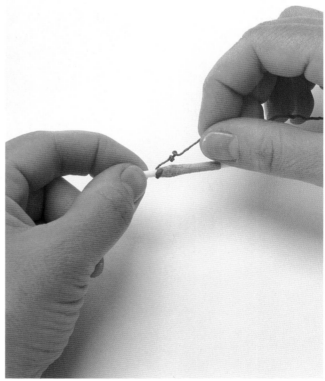

**1 Base**
Prepare a base of tissue. This sample uses the slim cylinder shape described for the colored tissue spiral.

**2 Tissue String Loop**
Glue a tissue string to one end of the base and wrap it around once. Wait for the glue to set, so the string is securely anchored, then twist the string until a loop forms.

### 3 Glue Loop
Put a dot of glue on the base and press the loop down onto it.

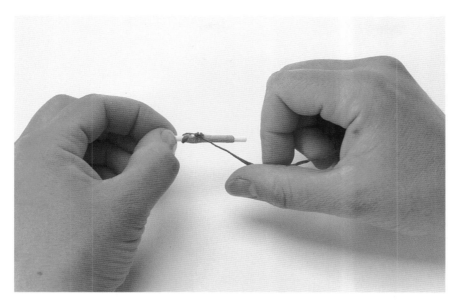

### 4 Continue Loops
Keep twisting and gluing more loops as you spiral toward the other end of the base. Hold down each loop as you proceed to the next to prevent it from popping off before the glue sets. At the other end of the base, wrap the string around once, trim off the excess and glue down the tip.

# CHAPTER SEVEN

# The Found Bead

**A**ny material flexible enough to roll around a small stick has bead potential. Chief among these is fabric, which can be handled almost exactly like paper. A quick course through a closet, thrift shop or yard sale can turn up exotic colors, patterns and textures.

Fabric can be used to form most of the paper shapes described in this book. The subtle texture of the weave adds a dimension of interest to even the simplest shapes.

A good pair of scissors is a must. Blades used on paper may be too dull to cut through cloth fibers. Fabric glue isn't necessary. All the samples in this book use plain white glue. The same varnish used on paper will work here, but be sure to test it on a scrap. Remember, varnish can darken material and obliterate some contrasts, an effect that can be more pronounced on fabric than on paper.

For a first project, avoid very thin, flexible fabrics like silk. They can be difficult to work with, stretching out of shape and fraying. Start with a commonplace, relatively stiff fabric like the cotton or the cotton/polyester blend used to make dress shirts, aprons and linens. The sample here uses an old cotton bedspread.

## Steps for a Basic Round Fabric Bead

**1 Cut Fabric**
Cut a long strip of fabric. Fabric is less likely to stretch out of shape and fray if you follow its "grain," or direction of the threads, when cutting the strip. The geometric design of the fabric pictured here has lines that also follow the grain, providing another clue to cutting it correctly.

**2 Roll and Glue**
Cut the strip into a long isosceles triangle. Roll and glue it around a stick just like paper. Some amount of fraying is bound to occur so snip any loose threads off after the bead is rolled. Finish with several coats of varnish.

# Fabric Applique Bead

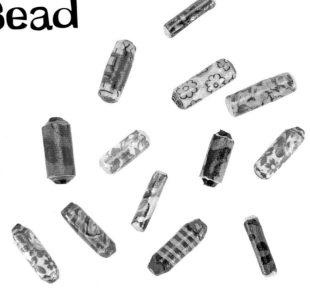

An applique over a paper cylinder base makes a quick and satisfying fabric bead. This method is particularly useful when working with thin, delicate fabrics that are difficult to manipulate on their own. It's also a good way to conserve a small supply of especially rare or meaningful scraps.

Fabric applique beads, as well as those made entirely of fabric, can be carved and tapered with a utility knife, just like beads made of paper.

## Steps for a Triangle Applique Bead

1. Make a slim cylinder base from a strip of paper.
2. Add a long isosceles triangle of fabric. In this sample, the fabric is thin silk from an old scarf.

## Steps for a Cylinder Applique Bead

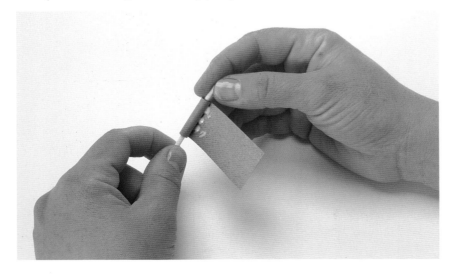

**1 Cylinder Base**
Make a slim cylinder base from a strip of paper.

## 2 Prepare Fabric Strip

Cut a strip of fabric. The cylinder applique works well with small, highly detailed designs like the flowers in this scrap from an antique apron. Trim the strip so the most desirable part of the design—a cluster of red flowers here—is at the end. Check the length of the fabric strip by wrapping it—not gluing, yet—around the paper cylinder base. Trim the strip, to take the best advantage of the design. Here the strip is given a curved end to follow the general shape of the flowers.

## 3 Roll and Glue

Roll and glue the fabric strip around the cylinder base.

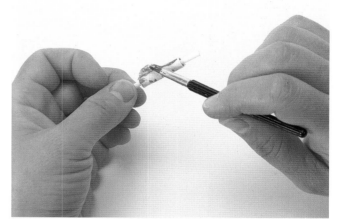

## 4 Glue End

Glue down the end, following its contours.

## 5 Finish

The bead can be left as a plain cylinder, or the ends can be tapered with a utility knife. A sharp blade will cut through fabric as easily as paper.

# Lace and Ribbon

Gain magnificent results in short order with these beads. Like fabric applique beads, the strength of the design rests on the beauty of the raw materials. Small, delicate, detailed laces and ribbons are a safe bet, but even the seemingly clumsy rickrack can be manipulated to transcend itself.

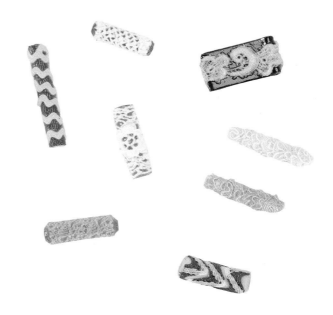

**Narrow Lace** Narrow lengths of lace can be spiraled around a paper cylinder base. In this sample, a brightly colored paper is chosen to contrast with the pale lace. Taper the ends of the bead with a utility knife after the spiral is complete.

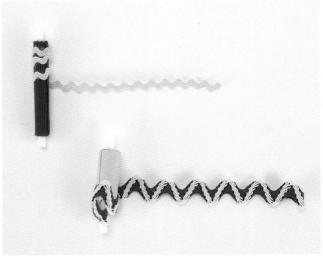

**Rickrack** Rickrack spiraled around a cylinder base generates a spare, flashy impact. In the top sample, the base is a length of grosgrain ribbon that contributes its own texture to the overall design. At bottom, the ornate purple and white rickrack rests on a base of plain construction paper.

**Lace with Centerpiece** In this sample, one layer of a 1″ (2.5cm) wide strip of lace is applied over a paper cylinder base. The strip of lace has been trimmed to leave the centerpiece of the design—a raised flower—intact. Although the lace alone produces an interesting bead, its intricate texture is also an ideal surface for painted decorations.

# Yarn

Colored yarn can be treated almost exactly like strings of tissue paper. The salvaged remains of old sweaters and socks can be used, but for the beads shown here I fell to the temptations of the colorful array of inexpensive embroidery floss at the local craft shop.

When working with yarn or floss, anchor the bead with a slim base of tissue paper as described in chapter six. This provides a secure foundation for gluing and winding the featured materials. If you're using a stick that will be removed when the bead is completed, a sturdier cylinder base of construction paper will be needed.

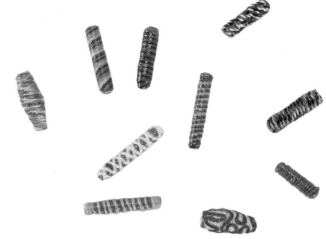

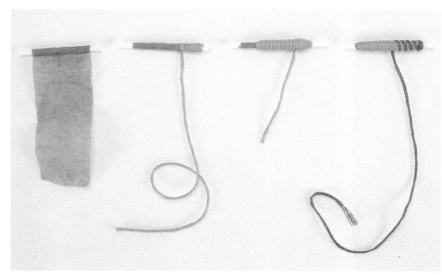

### Steps for a Yarn Spiral Bead

1. Make a slim cylinder base of tissue paper. (If the stick is to be pulled out, use construction paper.)
2. Glue the yarn to one end of the cylinder base. Begin spiraling the yarn tightly around the base.
3. Continue spiraling the yarn, going back and forth at least twice, to cover the base thoroughly.
4. Glue one tip of a contrasting color to one end of the base. Wrap it around the end once or twice, then spiral it toward the other end. Wind the spiral as closely as possible, while allowing the color of the base to show through. When it reaches the other end, wrap it around once or twice, glue it and trim the excess.

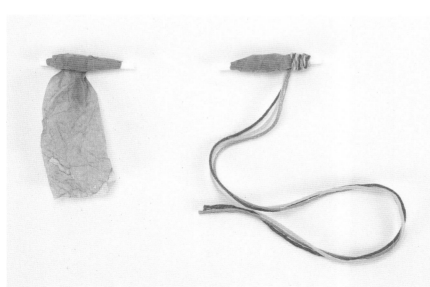

**Parallel Yarn Spiral** Another trick borrowed from tissue, yielding swift but dramatic results, is holding several different colors alongside each other and wrapping the group as one unit. Excess yarn can hang off the ends of the bead; it will be trimmed when the bead is tapered with a utility knife.

**Twisted Yarn Spiral** Like tissue paper, simple yarn spirals can be embellished in short order by twisting several colors around each other, and winding them simultaneously. This sample uses the shaped tissue base described in chapter six.

# Yarn Shapes

Yarn shapes, like their tissue cousins, have soft, textured contours that invite touching and holding. Intensely variegated shapes can be whipped out at high speeds by twisting several colors together, then wrapping them around a stick to form the shape. More complex designs must be constructed one element at a time.

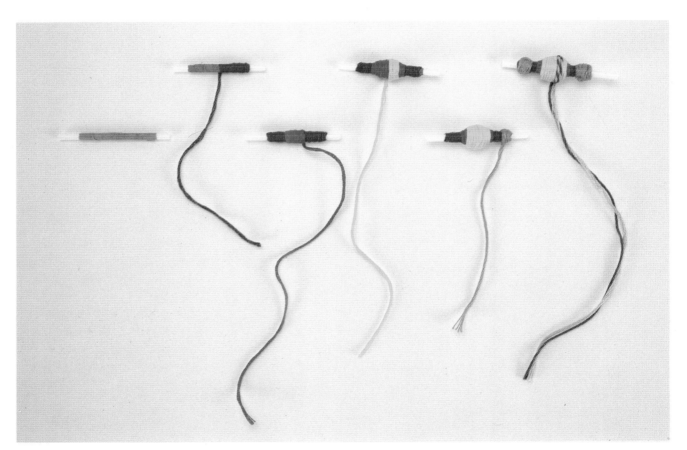

**Steps for a Complex Yarn Shape Bead**

1. Start with a slim cylinder of tissue paper.
2. Spiral yarn around the base tightly, making two or three even layers.
3. Using a contrasting color, add another two layers to the center of the bead. Leave equal amounts of the base visible on each end.
4. Add another color to the center, allowing just a small amount of the middle color to show.
5. At each end, wrap another color around seven or eight times, enough to build a small, round shape.
6. Highlight the center of the bead with a narrow strip of color. In this sample, it's made of two different threads twisted together, then wrapped around the bead.

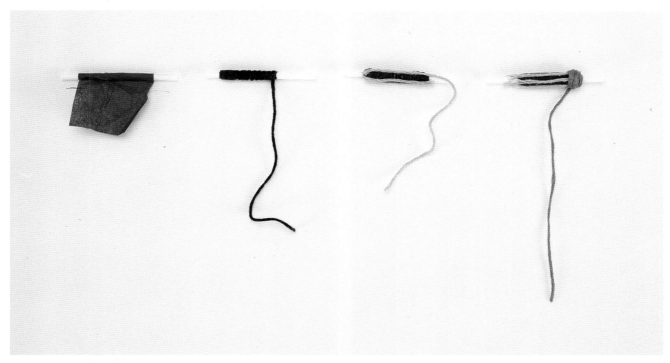

**Steps for a Yarn Shape with Applique Bead**

1. Start with a slim tissue base.
2. Spiral yarn around the base two or three times.
3. At close intervals, glue a contrasting color lengthwise along the base.
4. Using a third color, wrap yarn around each end, enough times to form a round shape.

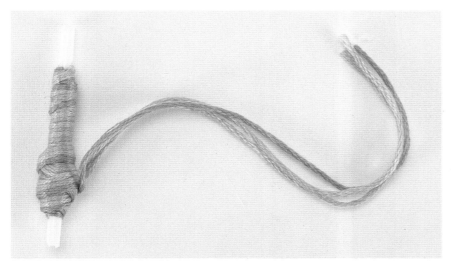

**Freehand Yarn Bead** For a freehand yarn shape, twist several colors around each other and wrap them together, piling up the layers unevenly to form a misshapen silhouette. This one is built on a slim base of tissue paper.

# God's Eye Bead

In miniature, many yarn based arts lend themselves to bead design. The God's Eye contributes new opportunities for stringing and arranging beads, because it has not just one hole, but two crosswise openings. The God's Eye has a front side and a back side, where any glue spots or loose ends may be hidden.

## Steps for a God's Eye Bead

**1 Cylinder Bases**
Make two slim cylinder bases. In this sample, they're made of tissue paper. Use a dot of glue in the middle to hold them crosswise and wrap yarn around the middle until it's firmly secured.

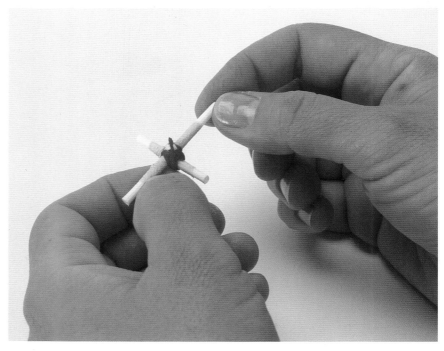

**2 Trim and Glue**
Trim off the excess yarn and glue down the tip. The glued side will be the back of the bead.

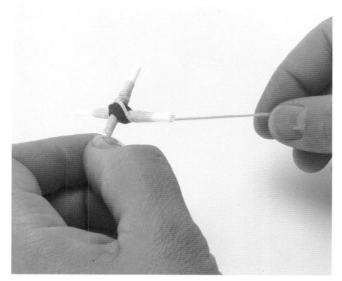

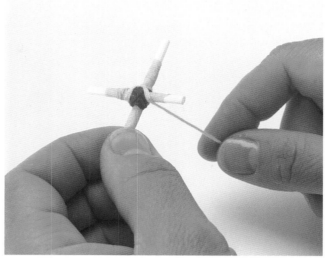

## 3 Contrasting Color

Glue the tip of a contrasting color to the back of the bead. Then turn the bead so the front faces you.

## 4 Loop Yarn

Start looping the yarn over, then under each of the four arms of the cross. The first round of loops should slightly overlap the bead's center, so there are no gaps in the bead's surface. Continue looping the yarn around and around the spokes, four or five times, to make a band of color about ⅛″ (.3cm) broad.

The front side of the bead has a continuous, flat surface. The back is divided into four segments by the arms of the cross.

## 5 Glue

Glue the tip of the yarn to the back of the bead.

# God's Eye Bead

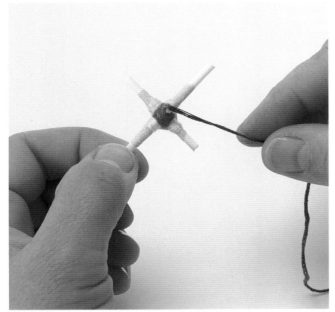

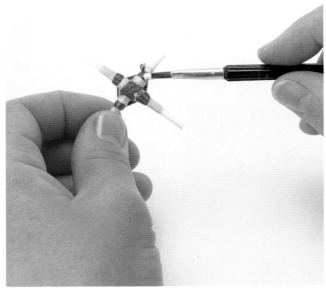

**6** **Another Color Yarn**
Glue a contrasting color to the back of the bead and loop it several times around the arms of the cross.

**7** **Trim and Glue**
Make a band of color and trim the excess yarn. Glue the tip to the back of the bead.

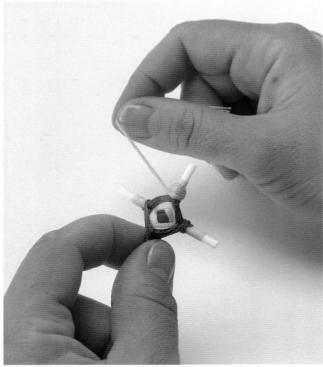

**9** **Trim**
Trim the excess ends of each arm to complete the God's Eye.

**8** **Another Color**
At the end of each arm, wrap another color around seven or eight times to form a small round shape.

# Flat Yarn Shapes

Construct these shapes by binding two, three or even more slim beads together. The yarns used to bind can be closely spiraled to form a continuous surface concealing the separate beads under it. They can also be spaced out or grouped together, allowing the underlying beads to display their colors.

## Steps for a Flat Yarn Bead

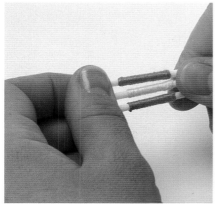

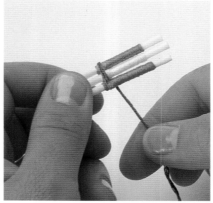

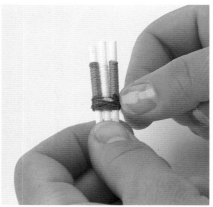

**1 Cylinder Bases**
Make three slim cylinder bases. Yarn is used in this sample but fabric or paper will work. These beads are made with a tissue base, spiraled over with two layers of yarn.

**2 Wind Yarn Around Bases**
Hold the three bases close together. Glue a contrasting color to one end of a bead and begin to wind it around the entire group.

**3 Form Band**
Continue wrapping the yarn around to form a narrow band of color at one end of the group. Trim the excess and glue down the tip.

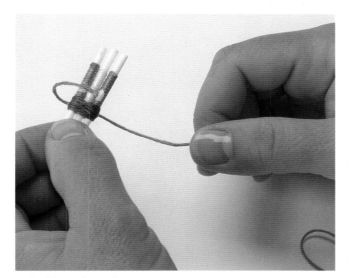

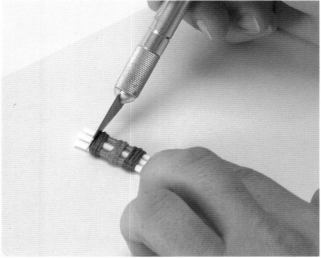

**4 Add Another Color**
Glue another color to the center of the group and wrap it around several times to form a band. Allow a stretch of the three beads to show between the new color and the first band.

**5 Finish Wrapping and Trim**
Wrap yarn around the other end of the group as in steps two and three and trim the ends.

# Painted Cotton Shapes

Cotton cosmetic puffs are ideal for molding into softly contoured shapes. The cotton absorbs paint beautifully, yielding bright, vibrant colors.

Puffs are actually long strips of cotton fibers rolled into balls. Before using the puff, pick along the edge with your fingertips to find the end of the strip and unroll it. Then the strip can be wrapped, twisted and glued, almost like tissue paper, to form a bead.

The beads shown here are made with 100 percent cotton balls. The large size is handiest, but smaller balls can be used. It's advisable to buy good quality because these are generally made with long cotton fibers. Lesser quality balls are made of short fibers, which disintegrate into shapeless fluff.

## Steps for a Painted Cotton Bead

**1 Unroll Puff**
Unroll a cotton puff into one long strip.

**2 Divide**
For ease of handling, divide the cotton strip lengthwise in half, making two slimmer strips.

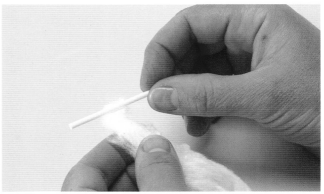

**3 Glue**
Glue one end of a strip liberally and place it against a stick.

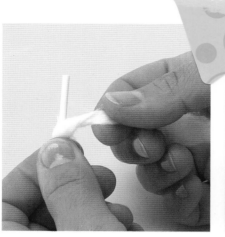

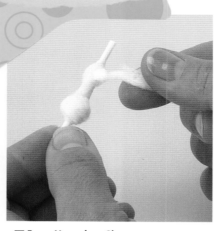

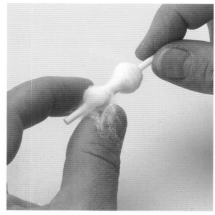

**4 Twist and Wrap**
Twist the strip slightly while wrapping it around the stick. Wrap it firmly, with generous amounts of glue, to make the bead hard and solid.

**5 Form Hourglass Shape**
To form an hourglass shape, twist and wrap the strip several times at each end of the bead.

**6 Layer Cotton Wisps**
Spin a thin layer of cotton wisps around the entire bead. This makes the surface of the bead smooth and firm and eliminates any stray glue on the surface, which could keep the cotton from absorbing paint easily.

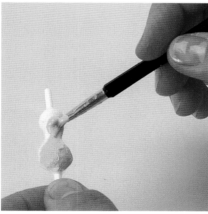

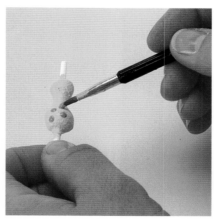

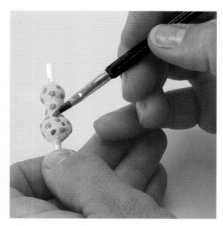

**7 Paint**
Coat the bead thoroughly with paint, allowing it to soak deeply into the cotton.

**8 Contrasting Color**
Wait for the first coat of paint to dry, then dot it with a contrasting color.

**9 More Detail**
Fill in between the dots with another contrasting color.

# Cotton Marbles

An exciting aspect of experimenting with a new material is discovering how to draw out its unique properties and apply them to new bead designs. The previous project treated cotton puffs almost like tissue, and now we'll turn to its ability to create an ethereal, cobweb-like pattern composed of wisps of thread.

Success here depends on the thickness of the paint used to color the wisps. If too thick, the wispiness may suffer under the weight of the paint. But if it's too thin and watery, the paint may feather into the base of the bead, undermining the delicacy of the pattern.

Tweezers are needed to draw out the wisps of colored cotton. I find it handiest to use a cotton swab soaked with paint, since I can hold it conveniently in one hand while constructing the bead in the other as shown here.

## Steps for a Cotton Marble Bead

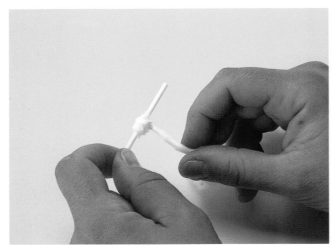

**1 Shape**
Make a round cotton shape on the stick.

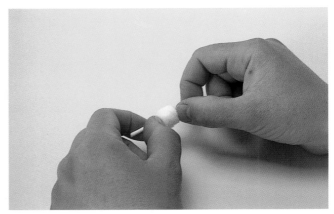

**2 Press and Twirl**
If necessary, firm up the top and bottom of the bead by pressing and twirling it between your nails.

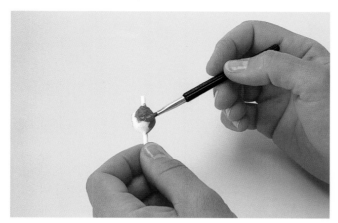

**3** **Paint**
Paint the bead thoroughly and let it dry.

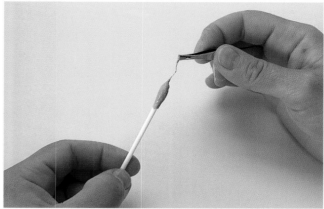

**4** **Create Wisps**
Soak a small wad of cotton, or a cotton swab, with a contrasting color of paint. While the paint is wet, pull out a wisp of cotton.

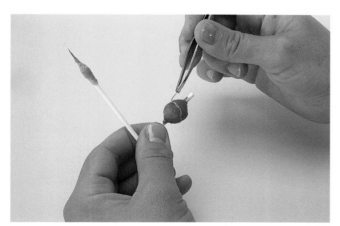

**5** **Drape Wisps**
Drape the wisp lightly around the bead. The wet paint will hold the wisp in place temporarily. After it dries, a coat of varnish will secure it.

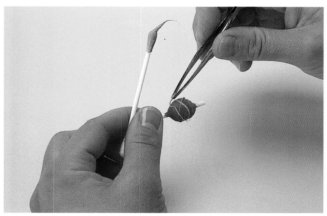

**6** **Finish**
Continue draping more wisps around the bead until the surface is covered to your liking.

# Gallery of Ideas

## Two Alligator Bracelets

Time is perhaps the most important factor in designing with handmade beads. Time becomes particularly urgent when your first bead is so magnificent you must wear it immediately, without waiting to complete the set.

This single-gator bracelet is a solution to that dilemma. After spending one day with my first alligator, I was so delighted with it that I whipped out a few tissue spiral beads to fill the bracelet and wore it that evening.

I strung the beads on colored telephone wire left behind by a repair crew. When I completed another gator, it only took a few minutes to snip apart the original bracelet and restring it with the new addition. Eventually, I got the bracelet I desired plus the pleasure of wearing it through all stages of its development.

To balance the design and give the gators some breathing room, a few small glass beads are interspersed among the handmade ones.

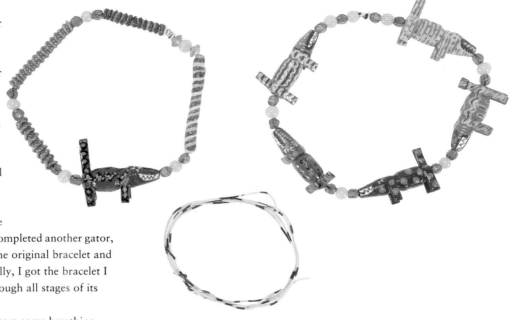

## Woman Earrings

Earrings are another design solution for the impatient craftsperson. Only two identical beads are necessary for a complete set; even one will suffice, depending on whether the body part with the hole in it comes in a pair or singly.

This set is based on the firecracker woman in chapter five. Instead of using zigzag trim to accent the layers of construction paper, I gave these ladies a softer style by applying cutouts from an antique paper doily.

## Disc Earrings

The disc shape shown in chapter three begs to show off the delicate spiral of construction paper that forms its broad surfaces. I separated the disc beads from each other with seed beads to expose the disc beads' best feature—their entire surface is open to view. Putting them adjacent to larger beads would obscure it. To gain an even better advantage, I string them on strands of standard beading wire instead of thread. The wire is sturdy but flexible. It can be bent easily to tilt the discs in different directions, allowing their surfaces to be regarded from all angles.

The side of each earring is decorated with a narrow strip of hand-cut zigzag trim.

## Tapestry Necklace

In the realm of the handmade, the designer's will is absolute. The same materials are used to make three types of beads for this necklace, all different in shape and size, a feat difficult if not impossible to achieve with manufactured beads.

These are construction paper beads decorated with cutouts from a brochure for an oriental rug company. The complex, flat geometric shape of the central bead, based on the monster bead described in chapter four, echoes the abstract patterns of the rug designs. Cylinder shapes fill out the necklace and frame the central bead, providing a broad canvas for the rug paper. The small shapes are basic round beads, accenting the ends of the necklace. Antique red and black glass beads provide the counterpoint.

## Pink Flat Bead Necklace

I usually start a jewelry project by conceiving a handmade bead, inspired by an interesting scrap of paper. When the handmade beads are complete, I shop around for the right manufactured beads to complement them. But for this necklace, the starting point was a small cache of antique beads. I designed the paper beads to complement them.

These paper beads show how the different techniques from the various projects and chapters can be combined in unique new ways. They're double flat beads made of construction paper, as described in chapter two. I engineered the two-tiered shape by layering a slightly narrower strip of paper several times around the completed double flat bead. This is the same method used for making the tiered round beads in chapter five.

I painted the tiered beads with a child's set of pearlescent paints and decided they needed more emphasis in the middle, so I layered on a long triangle. Using a method from chapter two, the triangle is made of typing paper, hand-colored with ¼" (.6cm) wide stripes using a child's set of glitter paints.

## Puppet Necklace

Pittsburgh in the 1970s didn't have bead shops—but it had a marionette company. Among the dim memories of my youth is one of being packed like a sardine into a small, hot theater with a horde of other excited children, then racing home to announce that I was going to be a puppet maker when I grew up. Innumerable career switches later, I finally made a puppet, and here it is.

This puppet is based on the Firecracker Woman from chapter five. To articulate the figure, I divided it into units: head (with hat), torso, legs, arms and hands.

Connecting the arms to the body in an attractive manner was a problem. My solution was to put holes in the shoulders using a variation on the double flat bead described in chapter two. The same strip of paper is wrapped around three sticks; the stick in the middle is for the torso and the outer sticks are for the shoulders.

## Beret

Cotton spiral beads allowed me to overdecorate my favorite hat, without adding to my burdens. The large beads are made with the cotton spiral method, as described in chapter seven. Besides the advantage of near weightlessness, they make a soft, pleasant clicking sound when they knock together.

Because they are on a hat, I knew these beads would be exposed to the elements at some point. To prepare them for the experience, I gave them four coats of varnish on the outside. Since I formed them around hollow plastic sticks, there was no need to varnish the insides; after trimming the excess stick, I touched up the ends with paint and varnish to seal the stick securely inside.

## Key Chain Charms

The length of a handmade bead is restricted only by the length of the stick upon which it is rolled. These beads are the longest that will fit on a plastic swab. The outsize proportions make them perfect for key charms, at least for people like me who can never find anything in their purses. I can always feel their unique surfaces.

Large as they are, the four beads pictured here required just a few scraps of origami paper. The bulk of the material is construction paper, with just one layer of origami paper interspersed in strategic surfaces. It's a useful approach for taking advantage of small scraps of particularly rare or expensive paper.

## Spools

How barren is the life of the modern child, now that wooden spools have gone the way of the dinosaur. Of course, the finer toy stores carry colored wooden spools boxed with their own shoestring, but the genuine articles, the ones that you can only get if you sew often enough to strip them of all their thread, are all too rare.

I love my paper bead spools. These are rolled around plastic drinking straws, providing a generously sized hole for shoestrings and pipe cleaners. Any of the beads described in this book can get a dimensional boost by using a plastic drinking straw or any large stick.

The classic spool shape is a cylinder framed by two disc shapes at either end. After making a number of spools, it struck me that paper beads can just as easily be adapted into toys for grown-ups. The piece shown here was intended to be the first of a chess set, but younger, more nimble hands quickly laid claim to it.

## Dolls

From oddly shaped spools, it's a short step to spools shaped like people. These figures are adapted from the Man and the Woman shapes described in chapter four and made of painted construction paper. They're formed around plastic drinking straws and can be strung like spools, but they also stand by themselves and can be played with like any other doll. Their proportions are similar to the small plastic, minimalist-style figurines popular with toddlers. They can be modeled to fit, like pegs, into the same cars, trucks and other accessories that their manufactured friends enjoy.

## Lapel Pins

These pins are made from flat beads rolled directly around the back bar of safety pins. This direct-to-jewelry method is described in more detail in chapter two. As with all flat beads, the surface allows almost any conceivable decoration.

## Oddments

Whether it's a silhouette that fails to spark, colors that don't catch fire or any other experiment gone awry, a beadmaking session often winds up with a few fellows just hanging about with nowhere to go. Having put heart and soul into their creation, sweeping them in the trash with the other scraps seems rather extreme to me, so I save them. Every once in a while I poke through them, find a few that don't look that bad after all, and string them together. In the necklace pictured here, they alternate with contemporary plastic beads.

# Index